The Penalty of Imprisonment

Louis Blom-Cooper

The Penalty of Imprisonment

Why 60 per cent of the prison
population should not be there

continuum

Published by Continuum

The Tower Building   80 Maiden Lane
11 York Road   Suite 704
London   New York
SE1 7NX   NY 10038

www.continuumbooks.com

First published 2008

British Library Cataloguing-in-Publication Data
A catalogue record for this book is available from the British Library.

ISBN 978-18470-6153-9 (hardback)

Typeset by Kenneth Burnley, Wirral, Cheshire
Printed and bound by Cromwell Press, Trowbridge, Wiltshire

Contents

Contents

Foreword

The mood and temper of the public in regard to the
treatment of crime and criminals is one of the most
unfailing tests of the civilisation of any country.

Winston Churchill

How society responds to crime and to its perpetrators has
been discussed in great depth by every generation. Ours is
no exception.

Too often the debate is characterized as offering only
a stark choice between being tough or soft. But to view
penal policy through this narrow prism misses the principle
that should be at its very core. Sentences should both punish and rehabilitate, not deliver one at the expense of the
other. The challenge we face as society in delivering an
effective penal policy is how best do we harness both these
elements and balance them appropriately.

In meeting this, it is vital we have a wide ranging
debate, away from emotive rhetoric and informed by
evidence of what works and when. History, as this book

points out, has much to teach us and we would do well to learn from it.

This book does not provide the whole answer, nor should it. Rather it argues we need to alter our underlying view of the purpose of our penal policy radically in order to tackle re-offending and reduce the numbers in prison. It proposes shifting the balance strongly in favour of rehabilitation not punishment.

As a society we need to come to a consensus and decide what we believe the mix between the elements should be. Some will agree with the balance this book envisages, others will not. For some it will go too far, for others it will not go far enough.

It is the Government's view that prison is, and will always remain, the right place for the most serious offenders, as well as for less serious offenders when other measures have failed or are inappropriate. But custodial sentences are not the only way offenders can be punished and rehabilitated. It is imperative that we have in place a rigorous and effective framework of community penalties which are used where they are the right course: penalties which not only punish but are effective in helping to tackle offending behaviour and reducing re-offending.

We remain committed to sentences, whether custodial or not, which deliver both punishment and rehabilitation. Whatever one's view – and I do not believe that the majority of the public want to see the radical shift in approach that this book envisages – this is an important debate and the book is a very welcome addition to it. And I remain in admiration of Louis Blom-Cooper's continued energy and engagement in this field.

The Rt Hon Jack Straw MP
Lord Chancellor and Secretary of State for Justice
January 2008

Preface

Some years ago, under the general title *The Penalty of Imprisonment*, I delivered the Tanner Lectures on Human Values at Clare Hall, University of Cambridge. My thoughts and concerns were shaped by the relentless increase in the amount and length of prison sentences and consequent incremental overcrowding of our largely outdated Victorian prison estate. Neither my interest in penal affairs* nor my concerns have diminished; on the contrary, as I have witnessed the persistent and pervasive impact of prison overcrowding on the lives of prisoners and on prison staff. Prisons and the penal system beyond them continue to operate in a state of crisis, to the detriment of the public interest.

When the numbers of prisoners exceeded the maximum capacity of our prisons, reaching in the summer of 2007 the daily average population of 80,000, I recalled my

---

*I was chairman of the Howard League for Penal Reform (1973–1984); a member of the Home Secretary's Advisory Committee on the Penal System (1966–1978); and a founder member of the Prison Reform Trust in 1981, and remained a trustee until 2001.

attempt to analyse the price being paid by a civilized society for the misuse of custody as the instinctive punishment for serious crime. Re-reading my Tanner lectures, I was acutely aware that nothing fundamental in the penal scene had changed; the lectures seemed to me to be as urgent and relevant as when I wrote them. Wishing to thrust them again into the public arena, I recognized the need to update them. This I have done and added a fourth chapter on the contemporary scene. Whatever the fluctuations in the rate of crime (official criminal statistics and the biennial British Crime Survey do no more than indicate imprecisely the true nature and extent of criminality) the inexorable contemporary response, in resorting to prison as the prime penal sanction, remains morally indefensible and operationally unsustainable, and even self-defeating. Restorative justice as a viable alternative method of dealing with some (if not the majority of) offenders is not yet sufficiently appreciated by politicians or the legislature. If (as I suggest) we have not yet developed the full potential of non-custodial penalties, the time has surely come when we really do mean what we say – prison is the last resort. Imprisonment for other than those who must be kept out of circulation for fear of serious physical harm – much as we do in the mental health system – should cease. The prison system needs to be turned inside out. The political parties have shown themselves incapable of breaking out of a continuing spiral of bid and counter-bid to reassure the public whose concerns about crime and punishment they also inflame, with the assistance of an irresponsible tabloid press.

Reform can now be achieved only by an independent commission on criminal justice and the penal system. Its terms of reference should be to inquire into, and make recommendations about, the criminal justice and penal systems of England and Wales, having regard to the state and nature of criminal activity and society's response thereto; in particular, to examine the concepts and purposes of all forms of penal sanctions.

The newly-elected SNP government in Scotland has pointed the way forward. The Cabinet Secretary for Justice, Kenny McAskill MSP, announced in October 2007 a review by an independent prisons commission to investigate the purpose and impact of imprisonment in contemporary Scotland, to report by June 2008. This review is established against a background commitment by the devolved government in Scotland to reduce the number of people sent to prison and blocking the future entry of the private sector in the Scottish prison system.

Chapter 1

Gaols and Goals:
Setting the Trap

Of such Ceremonies as be used in the Church, and have had their beginning by the institution of man, some at the first were of godly intent and purpose devised, and yet at length turned to vanity and superstition: some entered into the Church by undiscreet devotion, and such a zeal as was without knowledge; and for because they were winked at in the beginning, they grew daily to more and more abuses, which not only for their unprofitableness, but also because they have much blinded the people, and obscured the glory of God, are worthy to be cut away, and clean rejected.

'Of Ceremonies, Why Some Be Abolished And Some Retained'. From the Preface to the Book of Common Prayer

Imprisonment as an instrument of man's control over his fellow creatures has existed from time immemorial; but as the State's prime weapon of penal sanction for serious crime, it is of comparative modernity. Throughout the

1

ages, the uses and abuses of imprisonment have increasingly obscured the purposes of social control, to the point where prison as the core of the penal system in a democratic society is highly questionable. Penological thinking is full of confusion, even if confusion of thought is not an ignoble condition. The question, given extra urgency by the chronic overcrowding of our prisons, is whether imprisonment should be 'cut away, and clean rejected'.

Overcrowding is perhaps the most obvious prison problem, although others, such as the denial of human rights and dignity, are of more fundamental significance. The fact that it is the former that immediately attracts attention only goes to show how the English give priority to pragmatism over principle. Overcrowding, moreover, is not just a matter of numbers, although a daily average prison population in 1987 of over 50,000, well in excess of the certified normal accommodation, tells its own tale.

Overcrowding contributes to the problems of control and security. It presents the prison administration with practical problems which no amount of ingenuity will turn away. Victorian prison cells, which were designed for both sleeping and work, are ample for single sleeping accommodation, but shared by three for more than 16 hours a day (sometimes 23) they are not merely inhumane but squalid. Until recently the presence of three chamber pots made the situation socially and hygienically indefensible. The provision of water closets in prisons was not ungenerous; the problem is allowing access to them for prisoners who are locked up. In new buildings there is an answer to this problem, as can be seen in prisons like Albany (with its system of electronic unlocking) and the new Holloway prison (where toilets are provided in every cell), but in older establishments a solution came tardily, mainly because of the prohibitive cost and the shortage of space for the prisoners during installation.

Overcrowding is also not just a problem of accommodation. It infects all the prison services – water supply, drainage, cooking facilities, workshop space, educational and recreational areas; in consequence both time and space for those necessary activities have become grossly inadequate. But 'high cost squalor' (as one prison governor described it) is not the only dehumanizing and defeating aspect of imprisonment.

Human beings in prison face a loss of identity, the more so in the press of population. It is most marked among those who have to stay inside for long periods of time.

> Each day is like a year,
> A year whose days are long

So wrote Oscar Wilde in *The Ballad of Reading Gaol* (1897). To survive psychologically intact, long-term prisoners, above all, need to be relieved of the intolerable burdens of limited amenities and petty restrictions. The prospect of achieving this goal would be improved by lessening the time spent inside by minor and less serious offenders. Twenty-five years ago the number of life-sentence prisoners was only 200. In 1987 there were more than 2,000. In 2007, there are over 8,000. The painful process of adjustment to indeterminate sentences presents a constant threat to staff–inmate relationships; it is no accident that the most serious unrest has not been in the overcrowded local prisons, but in the long-term establishments, where, despite better physical conditions, the psychological pressures are more intense.

The whole prison scene is bleak. Many prisoners actually prefer the shared cell; for those who lack inner resources, the companionship of others is to be preferred to the solitariness of the single cell. But for most, the enforced close and intimate relationship is barely a mitigation of the hardships endemic in prison. The real pains of imprisonment are, of course, the boredom of everyday prison life, only partially relieved in the most favourable conditions, and the absence of choice, of freedom to seek privacy or companionship. The Victorian prisons, with their lofty halls, with cells opening onto lines of galleries narrowing in distant perspective, succeeded admirably in their unconscious purpose of reducing their occupants to insignificance. While modern prison building attempts to counter all this, it cannot remove the inevitable effects of imprisonment in diminishing the self-esteem (if they retain any) of those who are admitted.

The monotony in the small-scale pattern of existence and the lack of opportunities for acceptable expressions of tenderness in a rough masculine society are damaging, once the initial effect of such a jolt to ordinary habits of living has passed. Separation from partner and children disrupts family relationships and makes resettlement on discharge difficult. The serious disadvantage is that to live in any community is to be affected by its standards and attitudes, and identification with a criminal community means a rejection of those of normal society. For the recidivist prisoner the continuing round of conviction, imprisonment, release and reconviction, like a revolving door, is a process both familiar and perhaps inevitable. For society the essential task is to limit prison's defeating consequences, both in the prison setting and on release; but that is a task which prison staff find daunting, dispiriting and indeed impossible unless the numbers in prison are severely cut and the support after release considerably improved. Any moral satisfaction society may feel imprisoning the offender has to be set against its true cost in suffering to the offender and to his family and the not inconsiderable cost in maintaining him, estimated to be about £35,000 a year. It is not a question of whether the offender 'deserved' the punishment, but of its counterproductive consequences. These factors present the very strongest incentive to any society to limit, and as nearly as possible to abandon, the use of imprisonment. In a state of overcrowding, the incentive should be overwhelming. How is it then that as a society we have become so ineluctably wedded to an institution so palpably ineffective and inhumane?

The history of social control is the history of the struggle to reduce the use of violence, both between individuals and inflicted by the ruler or the state upon citizens. From the blood feuds of the house of Agamemnon to the duels of relatively recent times, it has been recognized that private vengeance undermines society and wastes lives. William the Conqueror abolished the death penalty, and through the centuries mutilation, branding, ducking stools and other punishments ranging from the barbarous to the degrading have been abandoned. Although capital punishment meanwhile was reintroduced, its deterrent effect was far from certain. Then, as now, the most professional offenders had a realistic assessment of their chances of not being caught at all; then, as now, the more severe the punishment, the more determined people were in trying to avoid it. Many juries and even law enforcers recoiled from applying it. Daniel Defoe, who had been imprisoned and pilloried (literally) in 1702–03 by the Tory government for his satirical pamphleteering, captured the way in which punishment makes the malefactor think not of his (or her) victims, but of himself: in *Moll Flanders* (1722) the heroine, in Newgate awaiting trial, says: 'I seem'd not to Mourn that I had committed such Crimes, and for the Fact, as it was an Offence against God and my Neighbour; but I mourn'd that I was to be punish'd for it'. The death penalty was progressively abolished, first for larceny from the person in 1808, and then for the other 200 offences for which it was then permissible, except murder, treason, piracy, and arson in Her Majesty's dockyards; these were the only capital crimes remaining in 1861. Several civilized countries abolished it in the nineteenth century, but it took until 1965 for the United Kingdom to rid itself of the death penalty for murder.

But (to revert to the eighteenth and early nineteenth centuries) a replacement for the death penalty had to be found. At first the solution was transportation – to the American colonies until the War of Independence; then, until 1867, to Australia. Until this period gaols were used primarily as a staging post – for prisoners held awaiting trial, execution at Tyburn, or transportation to the colonies. There were a few houses of correction and bridewells, mainly for vagrants and the unemployed, rather than for felons; they were intended to aid the poor and destitute as well as to correct the idle and dissolute, which shows that the tradition of trying to do two incompatible things at once in custodial institutions has a long history. It was not until the Australian colonies began to refuse entry to any more convicts that once again a replacement had to be found. This time the solution was internal banishment: lacking a Siberia, the Victorians adapted their prisons to a new purpose. Thus imprisonment as the ultimate penal sanction became an accretion to the law enforcement system and not just a method of temporary containment pending death or transportation.

Often, indeed, criminal process and punishment were not even used, but held in reserve. In medieval times, when prosecution was in the hands of the victims, they often preferred to bring a civil action to obtain compensation,

7

because if a felon was prosecuted and convicted his property was forfeited to the Crown. Similarly, in the eighteenth century, people of substance relied mainly on the *threat* of prosecution, which would be withdrawn in return for confession, restitution and apology. An early instance of restorative justice? Not infrequently, the victim was the master and the offender his servant, and the latter's dependency was reinforced by this apparent clemency. But as the prosecution was taken over by governmental authority (in practice the police), the victim was left with no part to play, except reporting the offence and possibly giving evidence. In essence it was a bargain, whereby the State accepted responsibility for dealing with offenders in return for the victim foregoing any claim to self-help.

Already reformers and others had turned their attention to gaols. George Fox, a Quaker imprisoned for his religious beliefs, saw at first hand in the mid-seventeenth century that prisons were universities of crime. Toward the end of the eighteenth, John Howard (1792) found the same, but concluded that the cure for communal squalor was the single cell. He recognized, however, that prisoners should be able to see the rules under which they were kept and that there is 'a way of managing some of the most desperate, with ease to yourself, and advantage to them', a truth which has been glimpsed at intervals ever since. The system must be based on the values it upholds. The philosopher, Jeremy Bentham, taking a wider sweep, recognized that all punishment is evil; unfortunately, he thought that it was justifiable, and possible, to use the evil to induce people to be good. His ideas were enshrined in the Millbank Penitentiary; but they didn't work. Under the Reverend Daniel Nihil as governor, 'the most successful simulator of holiness became the most favoured prisoner, [so that] sanctified looks were . . . the order of the day, and the most desperate convicts in the prison found it advantageous to complete their criminal character by the addition of hypocrisy' (Mayhew and Binney 1862). Many of those who could not adapt to the rigid and artificial regime went mad; for this and other reasons Millbank became one of the few major prisons ever to be demolished. (Tate Britain, built with sugar slave money, now stands on the site.)

In 1817 the Quaker Elizabeth Fry began her work of educating women prisoners. For those destined to be executed, this provided only a more humane way of passing their last days; but for those who would return to society, there was conflict between her goal and methods and those of the courts. Sentences were intended to punish and coerce; Mrs Fry had no power to punish, and she kept discipline by persuading the prisoners to agree to rules and by rewards. She was not able, in the prevailing climate of opinion, to make the consequential point that, if what the offenders needed to persuade them and enable them to live law-abidingly was education, prison was not the most suitable place to provide it. Alexander Maconochie was to encounter a similar conflict of aims: as governor of the remote penal colony of Norfolk Island in the 1840s, he devised a system of marks, by which prisoners could earn early release by good behaviour, and he promoted patriotism by giving them a good dinner on Queen Victoria's birthday. The reconviction rate went down; but his political masters wanted their convicts punished regardless of consequences, and he was recalled. Two years later floggings, and riots, returned to Norfolk Island. Returning to England, he became governor of Birmingham prison and introduced the marks system, but after another clash with his violently punitive deputy governor and the local justices, he was forced to resign.

Rehabilitative efforts were not always so humane. Reformers were trying to come to grips with the fact that prisoners learned criminal ways from each other; the more optimistic even believed that by a regular regimen, removed from the corrupting influences of the real world, offenders could be reformed. In America in the 1820s and 1830s, this led to the Pennsylvania and Auburn penitentiaries. Both involved silence; under the Pennsylvania system isolation was almost total, while at the Auburn prison in New York State, it was modified to the extent of allowing prisoners to work together – but without conversing or even exchanging glances. Discipline was enforced with the whip in Auburn, the iron gag in Pennsylvania, cold showers or the ball and chain elsewhere. Not for them Maconochie's insight that to accustom offenders to yield to external pressures was the opposite of what was required when they returned to face the world. The Quakers who devised these methods had at least paused to ask what was the purpose of the prison; but they left out of account that few people are rehabilitated through silent penitence – except Quakers.

Such were the theories in fashion (and fashion often has more to do with penal policy than reason or experience, let alone humanity) when the end of transportation was in sight and the first of the new wave of Victorian prisons was built at Pentonville in 1842. Solitary confinement was literally built into the design. Elizabeth Fry's last public protest was against these cells, which even had opaque ground-glass windows – though at first they did have sanitation. But in vain: more than 50 warehouses for the living dead were built by the end of the century. They have become, quite literally, monumental mistakes. A strict centralized regime was introduced in 1878; the Home Office began, as it meant to continue, by removing the independence of the previously outspoken inspectors, and the commissioners withheld reports from publication on the grounds that that would 'seriously impair their dignity and prestige and weaken their administration'. Although the rigours of the regime had to be moderated because so many prisoners became insane, as late as 1877 the incidence of insanity among prisoners apparently sane on admission was still admitted to be at least three times that in the general population; according to one estimate the proportion in local prisons doubled to 226 per 10,000 in the 15 years after the introduction of a strict centralized regime in 1878. The suicide rate among prisoners in 1877 was as high as 17.6 per 1,000; the problem was still acute in 1890, with many prisoners leaping from the upper landings, and the authorities at last responded – not by altering the regime, but by putting up safety netting.

The Victorians did not believe in idleness. Early in the century prisoners were often gainfully employed; but finding work was difficult for the authorities. Hence the invention of the crank and the treadwheel. The former could be installed in solitary cells; the prisoner was required to turn it several thousand times to obtain each meal. The uselessness of the toil enhanced the punishment. Some cranks lifted sand which was then dropped; others drove a fan above the prison: 'grinding the wind.' This method of punishment gave rise to an early example of penal policy by misleading metaphor: 'grinding rogues straight.' The policy assumed that prisoners were in some way morally 'warped', rather than responding to the poverty of the nineteenth century; even if that were accepted, grinding as a means of rectifying the problem would be about as much use as grinding a warped gramophone record; that is, it destroys what needs to be preserved: loyalty, respect, self-esteem, the desire to work, even the ability to work. To quote Wilde's *Ballad of Reading Gaol* again:

> Something was dead in each of us,
> And what was dead was Hope.

A more modern metaphor describes the nineteenth-century prison system as a social dustbin, or a massive machine for the promotion of misery.

How long to languish in gaol?

A perennial problem with time-based sanctions is determining how long they should last. An Act of 1717 which gave statutory force to the practice of transportation fixed the term at seven or 14 years in all cases, and this practice was followed in successive statutes. The only apparent basis for these terms was that seven is a number symbolizing completion or perfection, particularly in the Bible: there were seven sins in Talmudic law, and the Menorah (the candlestick representing Israel and used in Jewish worship) has seven branches. The Bible also calls for debts to be extinguished after seven years and for people to forgive 'unto seventy times seven'; but forgiveness has never been accorded a prominent place in criminal justice, although 14 years became a favourite maximum penalty on the statute book.

Terms of transportation were, by piecemeal changes to the law, converted to penal servitude in the mid-nineteenth century, and new penalties were introduced; judges were given more discretion in statutes laying down maxima rather than fixed penalties. But the five Acts of 1861, which formed the core of the modern criminal calendar, merely consolidated the confused existing position and did not attempt to grade the punishments in proportion to the seriousness of the crimes. Indeed, property offences tended to carry severer punishment than most offences of violence. Sentences of penal servitude were almost all for five, seven, ten years, or life, and few, if any, for six, eight, or nine. Further legislation, such as the Security from Violence Act of 1863, passed after the panic reaction to garrottings in London, did not improve matters, and the inevitable inconsistencies between judges led to further confusion.

A further problem was that sentences were widely considered too long. Even the hard-line chairman of the Prison Commission, Sir Edmund du Cane, wrote that 'every year, even every month and every week to which a prisoner is sentenced beyond the necessity of the case, entails an unjustifiable addition to the great mass of human sorrow'. He argued that it was possible to cut sentence lengths and thus reduce the amount of unnecessary hardship to prisoners and their families without any loss in the efficiency of the law. The Home Secretary, Sir William Harcourt, urged the Lord Chancellor in 1884 to convey to the judges the view that 'the deterring and reformatory effect of imprisonment . . . would be as well and even more effectually accomplished if the average length of sentences were materially shortened'. One person who rebelled against unnecessary severity was Charles Hopwood QC, a Liberal Member of Parliament, a barrister and the Recorder of Liverpool. Before his appointment in 1886 the average length of sentence was 13 months and six days; by 1892 he had reduced it to two months and 22 days. He gives an example: 'A poor woman pleaded guilty before me, charged with stealing a duck. I looked at her record. She had already endured, for stealing meat, 12 months'; again, for stealing butter, seven years' penal servitude; for stealing meat, seven years'; again, for stealing meat, seven years'; or 22 years of sentences for stealing a few shillings' worth of food! My sentence for the duck was one month, and I regret it now as too much. I have never since seen her.' His leniency did not unleash a crime wave, although it received a lash of the tongue from the local magistracy. He was able to quote the report of the Chief Constable of Liverpool to the Watch Committee in 1891, that never since the first returns of crime were published in Liverpool in 1857 had the statistics disclosed so small an amount of crime; compared with the previous year the number of indictable offences had decreased by 21 per cent, burglaries by 37 per cent, and serious crimes of violence by 42 per cent. 'Of course,' he adds wryly, 'I do not claim the credit of the decrease, although doubtless I should have had the discredit of the increase, had there been one.'

It was beginning to be recognized that imprisonment was not the only choice. As long ago as 1841 John Augustus had begun his voluntary work in the Boston Police Court, which developed into probation. The Police Court Mission began similar work in England in the last quarter of the century. William Tallack of the Howard Association, in a pamphlet in 1881, saw its potential and urged its introduction into the official system; the Probation of First Offenders Act was passed in 1887 and the more comprehensive Probation of Offenders Act 20 years later. Tallack was also among those who spoke at various international congresses of the rightness of reparation by the offender to the victim, but at that time the idea foundered on the problem that most offenders had no money.

Re-think or double-think?
The Gladstone Committee

By the 1890s, then, there was a fair amount of experience for those willing and able to see it. Locking people away, whether they are herded together or kept in inhuman isolation, is not very effective at changing people's behaviour on their return to freedom. Long sentences work no better than short ones, and perhaps worse. Punishments intended to deter are also not very effective. Even if they are indeed terrifying, people do not necessarily react as intended; they often do not think of the punishment until after they have committed the crime and are then devious in trying to avoid it. Brutal punishments brutalize (both the punisher and the punished); people respond to fair treatment; fairness does not exclude firmness.

But the central feature that was not appreciated was the conflict among the aims of the law enforcement system. If the main method of inducing people to obey the law is to threaten grim punishments, the effect on those individuals who are caught is often either to destroy them or to make them antipathetic to society. Probably the majority of hardened criminals is hardened in prison. Conversely, to treat offenders in the way most likely to persuade and enable them to be law-abiding will not terrify the remainder. This problem also determines the day-to-day administration of penal regimes. A policy of harshness encourages those members of staff who take pleasure in asserting power and inflicting pain; but an administration which aims to be fair and humane brings out the natural tendency of the majority of staff to treat those in their charge decently and help them as best they can – which makes the prison less terrifying.

In the early 1890s the harsh tendency was in the ascendant. The chairman of the Prison Commission, Sir Edmund du Cane, was not an inhumane man, but his system embodied a rigid combination of punitive deterrence and efficiency. This policy was publicly challenged by the chaplain of Wandsworth prison, the Rev W. D. Morrison. (The Official Secrets Act, which inhibits today's prison staff from exposing abuses, was still in the future; Morrison was, however, dismissed soon afterward for rashly speaking out in public.) Morrison wrote in *The Nineteenth Century*, the *Fortnightly Review* and *The Times*, and is credited with a series of articles in the *Daily Chronicle* in January 1894. The silent and separate system, imposed on prisoners, was described by Morrison as 'torture', especially for less hardened prisoners; prison inspectors reported to the chairman of the Commission, not to the Home Secretary; the staff were underpaid, overworked, and badly selected; there was, he wrote, a 'complete and utter breakdown of our local prison system'. Yet 'the great machine rolls obscurely on, cumbrous, pitiless, obsolete, unchanged'. The articles, and the paper's leader column, called for a Royal Commission; the following year H. H. Asquith, as Home Secretary in the Liberal administration, appointed a departmental committee with his under-secretary, Herbert Gladstone, as chairman.

The evidence presented to the Gladstone Committee, and its report, reflected a widespread revulsion against the inhumanity of the philosophy of deterrence, aggravated by the centralized control instituted by the Prison Act 1877. It drew from the head of the Home Office, Sir Godfrey Lushington, the statement that:

> I regard as unfavourable to reformation the status of a prisoner throughout his whole career; the crushing of self-respect; the starving of all moral instinct he may possess; the absence of all opportunity to do or receive a kindness; the continual association with none but criminals . . . ; the forced labour and the denial of all liberty. I believe the true mode of reforming a man, or restoring him to society, is in exactly the opposite direction to all of these . . . But of course, this is a mere idea. It is quite impracticable in a prison. In fact,

the unfavourable features I have mentioned are insep-
arable from prison life. (Prisons Committee 1895,
para 25)

Even Sir Edmund du Cane described imprisonment as 'an
artificial state of existence absolutely opposed to that which
nature points out as the condition of mental, moral and
physical health'.

The logical conclusion from such testimony would have
been that it was not in the public interest to send people to
prison, except for individual offenders who were a clear and
serious danger to the public. The risk of exposure to less
serious offences may even be increased by imprisonment,
after which there is a high rate of re-offending. A subse-
quent study found that of 2,568 men undergoing penal
servitude on a given day, 1,124 (44 per cent) had been
sentenced to that penalty before; if local prisons were
included, 1,546 men had been convicted six times or more.
The Committee published figures showing how the probability of a further prison sentence increased with each term
of imprisonment from 30 per cent after the first time to 79
per cent after the fifth. So much for individual deterrence!
But the Committee's remit was to study prisons, not
sentencing.

The report of the Committee (in 1895) was, by common consent, a landmark. Condemning separate confinement, it recommended more association for work and
instruction, relaxation of the silence rule (though talking

was still regarded as a 'privilege'), a distinct regime for juveniles in prison, and separate treatment for drunkards. But above all it introduced rehabilitation as a primary aim: 'the system should be made more elastic, more capable of being adapted to the special cases of individual prisoners; that prison discipline should be more effectually designed to maintain, stimulate or awaken the higher susceptibilities of prisoners to develop their moral instincts, to train them in orderly and industrial habits and whenever possible to turn them out of prison better men and women, both physically and morally, than when they came in' (Prisons Committee 1895, para 25). Sir Edmund du Cane retired and was succeeded by Sir Evelyn Ruggles-Brise. In 1898, with the passing of a new Prison Act, the crank and the treadwheel were abolished, remission (of one-sixth of the sentence) for good conduct was introduced, and the Secretary of State was given power to amend the rules for the treatment of prisoners without seeking fresh legislation. It was found that greater humanity led to 'quieter and more amenable' prisoners. The probation system was greatly strengthened in the Probation of Offenders Act of 1907, which also introduced in a small way the principle of compensation by offenders to victims; and the Borstal system, introduced in 1900, was confirmed in the Prevention of Crime Act 1908.

At last a serious, but unavailing, attempt had been made to break out of the trap in which law enforcers had become imprisoned by the dead weight of tradition. A new principle had been officially introduced. But there was a snag: the old one had not been discarded. The new era following the Gladstone Committee was based on deterrence combined with rehabilitation; and the inherent contradiction, and indeed conflict, between the twin philosophies have continued ever since, even if in an attenuated form.

The effects of the new climate took some time to show themselves. As regards those who passed sentence, the number of men and women they sent into local and convict prisons fluctuated above 150,000 a year from 1879 until 1913, with a peak of almost 200,000 in 1905. The daily average prison population declined somewhat after 1879, indicating some shortening of average sentence lengths. The number of offences punished by imprisonment fell from 139,000 in 1913 to 57,000 in 1914 and decreased further as the war went on; by 1917 the prison population was below 10,000. This was not entirely due to the emptying of the prisons into the trenches; in 1914 the Criminal Justice Administration Act allowed time for fines to be paid (as the prison commissioners and the Howard Association had both urged), and this reduced admissions by some 50,000 according to one estimate, with a further 25,000 attributable to increased employment and wages, which enabled fines to be paid. A further factor was the restriction of the consumption of intoxicants: normally, it was said, higher wages and convictions for drunkenness go together, but during the war they did not. The reduced use of prison does not appear to have endangered the public:

from 1905 to 1913 the number of indictable crimes recorded by the police only twice fell below 97,000; from 1913 to 1919 it never rose above 90,000.

The new emphasis on rehabilitation was adopted by the prison commissioners only with great caution. In their reports they stressed retribution and deterrence as well as 'reformation'. Whether or not one agrees with them, they deserve credit at least for spelling out their order of priorities. Retribution came first, and they were not impressed by 'loose thinkers and loose writers' who thought otherwise.

A special place in the political history of law enforcement belongs to Winston Churchill, Home Secretary in the Liberal administration in 1910–11. He was impressed by, among other things, Galsworthy's play *Justice* (1910), which depicted the effects of imprisonment and especially of solitary confinement. Both he and Ruggles-Brise were present at its first night. (Whether or not this was a case of *post hoc, ergo propter hoc*, is not certain.) He reduced the period of solitary confinement with which prison sentences then began (1911). On visiting Pentonville prison he was perturbed at the number of juveniles in prison for trifling offences, and 'with a view to drawing public attention in a sharp and effective manner' to this evil, he simply used his powers of executive release to free many of them early. The idea of a Home Secretary giving a 'short, sharp shock' to public opinion, rather than to young offenders, is an appealing one. He obtained a grant from the Treasury to pay for lectures and concerts in convict prisons (1909–10)

and appointed a committee on the supply of books to prisoners (1910). He extended prisoners' privileges (1910).
He urged the greater use of probation; and in regard to
prison sentences, a minute of his on a Home Office file in
1910 asks, 'Has not the time come for new maxima?' He
believed in the 'treasure that is in the heart of every man',
and with characteristic regard for language he warned:
'There is a great danger of using smooth words for ugly
things. Preventive detention is penal servitude in all its
aspects' (1910). Perhaps best known of all, he made a fine
declaration of principles which should underlie the treatment of offenders, at the end of his speech on the Prison
Vote (20 July 1910):

The mood and temper of the public in regard to the
treatment of crime and criminals is one of the most
unfailing tests of the civilization of any country. A
calm and dispassionate recognition of the rights of the
accused against the State, and even of convicted criminals against the State, a constant heart-searching by
all charged with the duty of punishment, a desire and
willingness to rehabilitate in the world of industry all
those who have paid their dues in the hard coinage of
punishment, tireless efforts towards the discovery of
curative and regenerating processes and an unfaltering
faith that there is a treasure, if you can only find it, in
the heart of every man – these are the symbols which
in the treatment of crime and criminals mark and

23

measure the stored-up strength of a nation, and are the sign and proof of the living virtue in it.

One significant effect of the war was the number of people imprisoned for offences newly created under the Defence of the Realm Act of 1916 and for conscientious objection to military service. Together with the women imprisoned from about 1905 onward for their activities in the campaign for women's suffrage, they included an articulate and influential group who would otherwise have been unlikely to see the inside of a prison or to believe prisoners' accounts of the regime. A committee was formed to collate their experiences and to inquire into the prison system generally. This they did with remarkable thoroughness, despite the refusal of the Prison Commission to provide information, to allow its staff to do so, or to supply a copy of Standing Orders. Fortunately, considerable evidence had already been collected from 50 prison officials; 290 ex-prisoners also gave testimony, as well as after-care workers and others. Published sources, such as the prison commissioners' annual reports, were fully used. The result, *English Prisons To-day*, was published in 1922, edited by Stephen Hobhouse and Fenner Brockway (later Lord Brockway).

This 700-page report is a detailed account of the prison system, scrupulously fair and free of rhetoric. It recorded some creditable aspects of the system and described some of the inhumanities which have now been abolished, such as leg irons, the convict crop (a convicted person's shaved head), and the broad arrow uniform. But it also gave details of the absence of industrial training, the lack of exercise, the practice of throwing excreta out of the window to avoid being locked up with it in the cell, the censorship of letters and the restrictions on visits, complaints of unsympathetic doctors obsessed with the prevention of malingering; there are harrowing accounts of prisoners lapsing into insanity and the use of 'observation cells' (in effect, solitary confinement) aggravating the mental condition of the suicidal. The unfair system for grievances is described, with a recommendation that the disciplinary function of Boards of Visitors should be separated from their role as a safeguard for prisoners against unfair treatment. Only in 1985 the Prior Committee had to repeat this procedure for reform. Reform had to wait a few more years.

The age of optimism

Suddenly a new climate prevailed. The year 1922 saw not only the publication of *English Prisons To-day* and the Webbs' masterly analysis, *English Prisons under Local Government*, but also the appointment of Maurice Waller as chairman of the Prison Commission – an appointment urged on the Home Secretary by Margery Fry. Alexander Paterson became a commissioner at the same time. Margery Fry also negotiated the merger of the two existing reform groups into the Howard League for Penal Reform, and became its first secretary. At that time it operated rather as a think-tank for a sympathetic administration; a later chairman of the Prison Commission, Sir Lionel Fox, was to describe it as 'Her Majesty's loyal Opposition to the Prison Commission'. The Commission quickly started to make reforms, improving the visiting facilities, informing prisoners of some of the rules, abolishing the silence rule, improving education: in short, reversing the priority from retribution to rehabilitation.

The new spirit was most marked in the Borstals, under the inspiring leadership of Alexander Paterson. Discipline was based less on any particular system or on punishment, more on education and personal influence. Many of the governors were 'characters'. At Huntercombe, Sir Almeric Rich would punish boys by making them pick up flints from the field – and did it himself alongside them to show that he shared responsibility for their misbehaviour. If he put a boy in a punishment cell overnight he would stay in the next cell, to give moral support, if needed. Another Borstal governor, John Vidler, didn't exactly punish a boy for not working: he said that work was a privilege, and the boy wouldn't be allowed to work until he changed his attitude. After three days in a cell, with as many books as he wanted, the boy decided he'd rather work. The institutions were supposed to be based on public schools; their 'housemasters' were expected to be bachelors, and worked until 9pm, with a day off a week and a weekend a month. As preparation for their work, they were likely to be sent by Paterson to work in an East End settlement to learn at first hand, as he had done, the conditions from which many Borstal boys came.

A basic insight of the leadership of this time was that people respond to being trusted. The contrast is highlighted by two details of Borstal history. When the first institution was opened at the village of Borstal, near Rochester, in 1901, its original inmates were transferred there in chains. Thirty years later, led by another remarkable governor, W. W. Llewellin, a party of lads went from Feltham, near London, to Lowdham Grange, near Nottingham, to start the first open Borstal; they marched, camping en-route, and not one absconded. Later he took another party from Stafford to North Sea Camp, near Boston in Lincolnshire. After the war even the young IRA volunteer, Brendan Behan, refused a chance to run away from Hollesley Bay Borstal because he didn't want to let the Governor down. Between the wars, the proportion of ex-Borstal trainees who did not re-offend within two years was over 60 per cent; of those who have undergone youth custody (the present-day equivalent of Borstal), over 60 per cent *are* reconvicted, and over 80 per cent of 15 to 16 year olds.

In the face of these success stories it must be remembered that there was another side. First, Borstals could, until 1961, choose their customers, and so they received the most promising young people; many were first offenders and not the rejects of approved schools and detention centres in, respectively, the pre-war and post-war years.

Second, because of the glowing picture of Borstals at their best, painted by the reformers and the prison authorities, Parliament set a long period (originally three years, later reduced to two) for Borstal training; and it is virtually certain that courts often sent young people there who did not deserve incarceration, for the sake of the training. Unfortunately, they did not know that the training was very limited. There were allegations of brutality at some Borstals, one of which was later closed as a result.

For adults also there were some relaxations in the prison regime, a spillover from Borstal techniques. Educational facilities were improved, and in 1929 an earnings scheme for prisoners was started, at the suggestion of the Howard League and with the help of one of the Cadbury charitable trusts. The earnings of 8–10p per week were worth more, allowing for inflation, than prisoners receive today.

The improvements were far from universal. The grievance and disciplinary system criticized by Hobhouse and Brockway remained unaltered until the 1970s. Educational and other reforms were still regarded as something of a privilege. There were disturbances in Parkhurst in 1926 after cuts in the educational facilities, to which 85 per cent of prisoners had no access during the year – and in the 1980s cutbacks in education were again contributing to the tension in the prisons. In 1927 it was 'not thought necessary' to appoint prison visitors to Dartmoor and Parkhurst. In Dartmoor things were, if anything, worse. In 1928 there was no educational adviser and no definite intention of appointing one; there were only 19 lectures and 95 classes for young convicts in a whole year. The financial crisis forced a reduction of staff in prisons generally, with a cut in the working day to about five hours. In January 1932, after attacks on officers, there was a serious riot at the prison: the administrative block was set on fire, and police had to be called in to restore order. An official inquiry under Herbert du Parcq, KC (later to become a judge and a Law Lord) found, not for the first or the last time, that Dartmoor was unsuitable for use as a prison. The Home Secretary, Herbert Samuel, stood firm against those who said that courts and prisons were becoming too soft; as the *New Statesman* remarked, the trouble at Dartmoor could hardly be blamed on 'modern methods of prison treatment', since Dartmoor had remained almost untouched by them. Cicely Craven, the Secretary of the Howard League, similarly, wrote to the Home Secretary: 'The main criticism to be levelled against modern prison administration is not that there is an excess of leniency; but that there is stagnation.'

The situation was not helped by the sentence of 'preventive detention', introduced in 1908 with the intention of containing the 'professional' criminal; in practice, it netted mainly habitual petty offenders and incapacitated them still further for life outside. The Prison Commissioners, while still holding to the belief that prison could serve the double purpose of prevention and cure, did not think that lengthy periods of imprisonment would be long supported by public opinion, and they recognized that a man might be worse for prison experience and could leave with ideas of revenge upon the society that had deprived him of freedom. They concluded, however, that prisons should be improved, not that they should be abolished. A Departmental Committee on Persistent Offenders recommended the reform of preventive detention, the provision of adequate work in prisons, with payment of a proper rate for the job, and employment for ex-prisoners. Proposals were made to improve the effectiveness of the voluntary aftercare societies. As usual, part of the problem lay in employment conditions in the world outside prisons; and part was caused by the fact of imprisonment itself, which then required a great deal of further effort to mitigate its damaging effects.

The interwar period is nevertheless generally seen as one of progress; the prison population remained stable at about 11,000 for two decades, and in 1938 a Criminal Justice Bill was introduced, proposing the abolition of corporal punishment (which was already little used because courts recognized its ineffectiveness) and a reduction in the incarceration of young offenders through the establishment of hostels, to be known as Howard Houses. If a spectator of the penal scene at the outbreak of war could feel that further progress was simply being postponed, he would not have predicted anything radical. The penal system remained in essence what it had been since the abandonment of transportation. But, although much of the harshness had been removed and the idea of rehabilitation had been introduced, the twin philosophies in all their confusion persisted. There was no discernible escape from the ultimate penalty of imprisonment; the trap had been set.

Chapter 2

Conflicts in Criminal Justice: Caught in the Trap

By the time war broke out in 1939, it seemed as if progress was being made toward a more humane system of criminal justice and penal practice. The old barbarities had been largely swept away, and the institutions which replaced them were intended, in part at least, to be reformative. The prison population had been more or less constant for two decades, at about 11,000, largely owing to the increased use of probation. The Criminal Justice Bill of 1938 had been introduced, intended to reduce further the use of imprisonment for young offenders, replacing it by residence in Howard Houses (something like strict, but not necessarily punitive, probation hostels) followed by supervision. The Bill would also have abolished corporal punishment, except in prisons. But it had not completed its passage when war was declared.

The preservation of freedom and justice was high among the aims of those who fought in the Second World War, but from 1939 to 1945 it had to wait for its application on the domestic front: the conduct of the war itself had to take priority. The Criminal Justice Bill of 1938 was shelved, and little happened on the criminal justice front, apart from an increase in prisoners' remission for good conduct from a quarter to a third of the sentence as an expedient to reduce the prison population. A bill similar in most respects to the pre-war Bill, notably in abolishing corporal punishment, was introduced in Parliament in 1947. But the climate of opinion had changed somewhat, and the Howard Houses proposed in 1938 were replaced in the 1948 Act by detention centres which were explicitly punitive – the 'short, sharp shock' was the rallying cry of those intent on curbing juvenile delinquency, perceived as a growing evil. One reason for the change may have been the continuing rise in recorded crime figures: in the decade from 1928 to 1938 the number of indictable offences recorded annually increased by about 150,000; in the next decade it went up by about 240,000. There was much talk of the 'glasshouses' used by the Army, and no doubt a number of members of Parliament had had occasion to send misbehaving soldiers there; probably rather fewer legislators had been on the receiving end. Be that as it may, detention centres were introduced either to combat crime or to satisfy those who believed them to be necessary to make up for the abolition of corporal punishment, despite the evidence. Home Office research showed that flogging made men more likely to re-offend, so that simply to abolish it would make the public safer. As for 'glasshouses', little is known about their effectiveness, but the belief that men 'never came back for a second dose of the punishment' may be due to special factors, such as the accepted disciplinary ethos shared by those in the armed forces, and to the fact that many offenders were discharged from the Army, so that any future offending would not come to the notice of their former superior officers.

Optimism nevertheless prevailed. The proportion of offenders sent to prison continued to go down; in some years the numbers convicted of indictable offences, and even the prison population, actually decreased. In 1958 the First Offenders Act was passed; it had been promoted by the Howard League to try to discourage courts from sending an offender to prison for the first time. The Criminal Justice Act of 1961 required all young adults to be sent to Borstal if the court decided on custody for an intermediate term, and it actually gave the Home Secretary power to abolish the use of short sentences of imprisonment (six months or less for offenders under 21 years old) as soon as there were enough detention centres to replace the prison space otherwise used. But the power was never exercised: the Advisory Council on the Penal System's report in the 1970s was to herald its demise. It was also in a spirit of optimism that the Howard League pressed for research: the 1948 Act gave the Home Office power to spend money on research, and in 1959 R. A. Butler, as Home Secretary, was persuaded to establish the Cambridge Institute of Criminology. This coincided with the publication of *Penal Practice in a Changing Society*, a government publication that was redolent of hope for the future in prescribing means of reducing the reliance on imprisonment. It also, unhelpfully, heralded the burgeoning prison-building programme. Blundeston, opened in 1963, was the first prison built since Camp Hill (1912), whose construction had been authorised by Winston Churchill. There was still a feeling that with more knowledge of the causes of delinquency it would be possible, however, to find solutions. The idea of a scientifically based penal policy received a severe setback in the 1960s. A Royal Commission on the Penal System had been appointed; but a request from one of its members, Professor Leon Radzinowicz, the director of the recently established Cambridge Institute of Criminology, for substantial research backing along the lines of the US President's Commission was turned down. Two years into the Commission's work there developed a schism over penal philosophy. Unprecedentedly for a Royal Commission, it was dissolved and was replaced in 1966 by the Advisory Council on the Penal System with a remit to study specific topics. Meanwhile the Government, urgently concerned to reverse the growth of the prison population, turned to fresh legislation. The Advisory Council, over the next 12 years, produced a series of reports, largely designed to shift the emphasis from custody to non-custody. Despite this, or because of it, the Council was included among the 'quangos' discarded by an incoming Conservative administration of 1979 that did not want independent advice on penal matters – an attitude persisted in by successive administrations.

Mixed motives: detention centres

It has often been pointed out that sentencing practice might be very different if the courts were responsible for the budget from which their sentences have to be paid for. They are probably the only official agency which, subject only to trying to observe some degree of consistency, can pursue whatever policy its members like; they must observe maxima set by Parliament, but Parliament in doing so does not have financial considerations in mind and does not even have to provide an estimate of the cost of setting the penalty for any particular offence. There is another built-in conflict, however, identified in a Note of Dissent to the report of the Advisory Council on the Penal System's report *Young Adult Offenders* (1974). This is that the *goals* of the sentencers are different from those of the institutions to which they commit people. 'We send someone to school or hospital so that he may be educated or treated, and that is what schools and hospitals set out to do. But we send an offender to prison largely to deter him from further offences or to register society's disapproval of his action. But once he is there, we try to treat him. Only keeping the offender out of circulation is clearly common to both sets of objectives.' The contradiction is even more fundamental than the dissenter noted: a further major reason for sending a person to prison is supposedly to deter *other* people from offending.

An example of the contradictions inherent in a law

enforcement policy that is part punitive, part rehabilitative is found in the story of detention centres. The catchphrase used to describe them, the 'short, sharp shock', was another example of the misleading metaphor in penology: as Baroness (Barbara) Wootton pointed out, the Gilbertian phrase referred to decapitation. Some people in any case found three months a long, blunt shock. The motives for introducing detention centres (in the Criminal Justice Act of 1948) and their augmentation (in 1961) were, as usual, mixed. For some, they were a sop to buy off the opposition to the abolition of corporal punishment, and therefore had to be as much of a 'short, sharp shock' as possible; to others, they were a way of persuading courts not to send young offenders to prison – indeed, it was anticipated at least that they would replace imprisonment. At first, the greater problem was not that the staff's aims differed from those of the courts, but that they were too enthusiastic in achieving the punitive goal. From the establishment of the first centres in the 1950s, there were repeated complaints of pointless and degrading work and even of brutality. The prison crop, abolished in the 1920s, was reintroduced. The reception procedure was often a chilling, impersonal and humiliating experience. Visits were restricted and letters censored, as in prison. Solitary confinement and dietary restriction were used as punishments. Much of the work was deliberately hard and boring, such as separating old electric cables into their component materials – a modern version of oakum-picking, of which Hobhouse and Brockway remarked that 'the effect of attempting to make prison labour "deterrent" with a view to inculcating a distaste for prison is to make labour itself distasteful'. The same might be said of cleanliness, tidiness and routine. For girls, the regime was so obviously unsuitable that it was abolished, following a visit to the one centre by the Advisory Council on the Penal System and an immediate interim report to which the Home Secretary responded favourably.

Against this background, an attempt was made, in the Criminal Justice Act of 1961, to make the sentence more constructive by grafting on compulsory after-care; but there was still unease, and the Home Secretary asked the Advisory Council to report on detention centres. Without dwelling on the allegations of brutality, they made it clear in their report (1970) that the Bishop of Exeter (Dr Robert Mortimer) and his colleagues on the sub-committee believed in a more educative regime, including remedial education for the one in four of the intake whose reading age was ten or below. The teaching of illiterate boys to read was a marked feature of the programme for those under school-leaving age. The Advisory Council tried, optimistically, to square the circle by proposing that discipline should remain firm and the regime brisk and exacting but constructive; the punitive aspect of the detention centre should be limited to the deprivation of liberty. Within a year or two several centres were enthusiastically expanding their remedial education programmes; some used electric typewriters, then a new and expensive gadget, as a teaching aid. The militaristic approach had all but disappeared by the time the Advisory Council had reported; the centres had become little more than mini-Borstals, with the same constructive training, only shorter in duration. In 1974 the Council recommended a generic sentence of youth custody. It has taken two decades, via an absurd revival in 1980 of the 'short, sharp shock' philosophy, to reach that sensible objective in the form of the Young Offenders Institute.

In 1980 Lord (then Mr William) Whitelaw reinvented the wheel by introducing at two centres (and later two more) a 'brisker temp', hard physical work and physical education, less association, an earlier time for lights out, and more parades and inspections. This was called an experiment, as if the period of the 1960s had not itself been an experiment that had palpably failed. Mr Whitelaw had earlier admitted that he had no idea whether it would work. The 'experiment' was set up in a way that made clear evaluation impossible; nevertheless the research report, the publication of which was delayed until 1984, was able to conclude that there was no improvement in reconviction rates. Over half were reconvicted within a year, both in the experimental centres and in the rest. Worse than that, the 'trainees' disliked the work but enjoyed the drill and tough physical education – the opposite of the desired result.

The Home Secretary by now was Mr Leon Brittan, who had been the junior minister responsible for implementing the 'experiment'. He responded by extending tougher regimes to all detention centres – another setback for a research-based policy of criminal justice. The only lesson the politicians chose to draw from the research was that the drill should be stopped; they had missed the point that what mattered was not that it was strenuous, but that to do it correctly was an achievement. The boys were now back to tasks like polishing floors by hand; also an achievement of sorts, but since it could be achieved more appropriately by machine, their real achievement was keeping their tempers when they were made to do such unnecessary tasks. Some centres and individual prison officers subverted the punitive intentions of the politicians, as they had done in the 1960s, by introducing social skills courses and other educative activities. At other centres allegations of brutality began to surface once again. In one, prison officers even behaved in a humiliating way towards youths in the presence of prison inspectors. The chief inspector noted in his report for 1985 that for many of the staff 'there was an inherent tension between the demands, on the one hand, of the brisk physical regime and, on the other, of the need to care for inmates'. There had been a drop in the number of 14 to 16 year olds sent to junior detention centres; but courts were apparently sending at least some of the 15 to 16 year olds to youth custody centres instead. Whether this was because youth custody sentences were longer (over four months) or because, to a limited extent, they included some form of training, was not clear. But detention centres were all of a piece with a mischievous social policy that can now be consigned to the penal history museum, along with the rack and the thumbscrew.

The decline of rehabilitation

The Advisory Council saw from the outset that detention centres could not be thoroughly reviewed without rethinking the principles on which the treatment of young adult offenders was based, in the wake of the Children and Young Persons Act of 1969, which had done the same for younger children in trouble. The 1969 Act was the last major attempt to enact the rehabilitative ideal; it was based on the philosophy that many young people who offend have had a deprived upbringing and that society's response should be to allow social workers to help them overcome their disadvantages. The vagueness of this concept was reflected in its name, 'Intermediate Treatment'. Courts complained that, after making a care order, they were likely to meet the offender in the street a week later: another example of anecdotal penology. Without necessarily being punitive, they wanted to make sure that 'something' happened to the offender; this probably accounts for some of the increase in the use of detention centres in that period.

In 1974 the Advisory Council produced a thorough, sensible, but not very radical report, *Young Adult Offenders*, but it came too late to avoid the first financial retrenchment following the economic crisis. It recommended the abolition of detention centres and Borstals in favour of a

single, educative Custody and Control Order, with supervision after release; to encourage the use of non-custodial
sentences, a stricter one would be introduced, called a
Supervision and Control Order. The orders favoured
considerable use of discretion: in releasing inmates from
custody, and in detaining those on supervision for up to 72
hours on suspicion that the offender was contemplating
another offence. This idea was imported from America and
provoked fierce opposition, particularly from probation
officers: unlike their American counterparts, some – particularly the younger members of the service – saw themselves
primarily as social workers, rather than law enforcement
officers, and they did not want to become, as the catchphrase of the time had it, 'screws on wheels'. But by taking
on after-care, prison welfare, parole, and community service orders, the probation service had become an important
segment of penal practice. There was another problem
with the proposals: the catchphrase for this was 'widening
the net of social control'. This meant that whenever a new
measure was introduced intermediate in severity between
imprisonment and probation, with the intention of persuading the courts to use it in place of prison, the courts
would also tend to use it where probation would have been
adequate, as a sort of novel penal toy to which the judiciary
was magnetically attracted. Not only is this excessive in
itself, but, if the offender breaches the order, he is also
likely to be given a more severe sanction than for not com-
plying with a probation order. Thus he is doubly worse off,

and may even end up in prison for an offence which did not deserve it.

This effect was strikingly demonstrated in relation to adults, in the introduction of suspended sentences in the Criminal Justice Act of 1967, to be buttressed a decade later by the partially suspended sentence, introduced in 1976. In theory, fully suspended sentences were prison sentences, but only their symbolic value would be enforced; provided the offender was not reconvicted, he suffered only the stigma of the prison sentence, not its reality. But the courts frequently used the new power in place of lesser penalties; moreover, they did not think that stigma alone was enough, so they made up for it by lengthening the sentences that they suspended. Thus offenders who re-offended went to prison, and for longer than if suspended sentences had not been invented. After a temporary drop, the prison population rose at least as fast as before.

A second innovation in the 1967 Act was parole, and here again confused motives ultimately led to a system that became widely discredited in the eyes of penal reformers, prison administrators and staff, and prisoners, alike. It was partly an expedient to try to limit the prison population; partly an example of anecdotal penology. The White Paper *The Adult Offender* (1965) referred to tales told by prison governors, who said that they often recognized, in long-term prisoners, a 'peak of response' after which they (the prisoners) began to deteriorate. Parole is supposed to allow prisoners to be released at this peak. But the system is enmeshed in a tangle of contradictions. A Governor may recognize the 'peak' in some prisoners, but the chances were against a local review committee, let alone a remote parole board, being able to identify it in thousands of cases a year. Prisoners had to serve at least one-third of the sentence and, in the original scheme, a minimum of 12 months from the date of sentence before being eligible, so it was idle to reach one's peak before then. Also, there were extra criteria: parole depended not only on 'responding', but on the seriousness of the offence and on conduct while in prison; failure on any one of these criteria jeopardized early release. A fortunate offender with a home and job to return to was probably a 'better risk' than one without these advantages, and therefore stood an unfair chance of being released sooner. The offender who was a 'worse risk' was less likely to get parole and therefore was released at the end of his sentence without a period of supervision in the community. To meet this point some offenders were given parole early, to ensure that they did have some supervision; the others naturally regarded this as unfair. In November 1983 Mr Leon Brittan, as Home Secretary, added to the sense of unfairness by restricting parole for certain long-term prisoners; for short-termers, however, the minimum qualifying period was reduced. Unforgivably, Mr Brittan also withdrew two life-sentence prisoners from open prison and closed conditions so that the new policy would be applied to them. He received judicial upbraiding from the Master of the Rolls, Sir John Donaldson (later

45

Lord Donaldson of Lymington), when the policy was subjected, unsuccessfully, to judicial review. It was generally believed, though the courts denied it, that sentences lengthened to take account of parole.

The catalogue of contradictions is a long one; what it adds up to is that a fair system of parole is impossible, at least as long as there are several conflicting criteria, and members of the Parole Board, striving to be both fair and humane, have been attempting the impossible. (Attempting the impossible, however, is contemplated illogically by the criminal law. If, for example, I hand over a packet of tealeaves, thinking that it is cannabis, I am guilty of attempting to traffic in proscribed drugs.)

Above all, the system was designedly based on executive action, with no element of judicial review. Strasbourg, however, decided that on recall a prisoner is entitled to due process of law. That case provided the impetus for the setting up of a Departmental Committee to review the parole system under the chairmanship of Lord (Mark) Carlisle (himself a former member of the Advisory Council and a junior minister at the Home Office in the Heath administration). The unravelling of that penological knot still called for some ingenuity. Parole survives in an attenuated form, subject also to greater political control over the release of life sentence prisoners.

The great depression

By the late 1970s the earlier penal optimism was turning perceptibly to depression. Rising affluence and welfare benefits had not brought a reduction in recorded crime figures. Rehabilitative sanctions, including non-custodial ones, fell out of favour, although for different reasons. Courts felt that they did not work because they were too 'soft', besides having a tendency to transfer decisions about offenders from courts to social workers. Reformers began to take exception to the parole system by which a person could be deprived of liberty for 'treatment' purposes for a long time for a minor offence if he did not 'respond' – which could mean that he was not given any treatment to respond to or that he refused to submit meekly to prison regimentation. Even research, which liberal reformers had hoped would show how to reduce crime, fell from grace: surveys of research on rehabilitative projects which had appeared to show promising results served only to demonstrate that in many cases their design was flawed, so that their findings were inconclusive. A widely quoted American article by Robert Martinson, entitled 'What Works?' (1974), concluded, 'With few and isolated exceptions, the rehabilitative efforts that have been reported so far have had no appreciable effect on recidivism.' 'Nothing works' became a slogan which made a generation of prison staff and probation officers wonder if their jobs were worthwhile. The later 'Prison Works' underwent a similar

47

dismissive action. Predictably morale was low, never more so than in Borstals, where devoted staff became thoroughly disillusioned.

There were answers to these strictures, but somehow they did not attract attention. If research did not prove that a project had succeeded, that did not necessarily prove that it had failed. Projects which spelled out clear and specific goals, such as teaching literacy or social skills, stood a fair chance of success. Martinson's own findings did not justify his conclusions; indeed, a few years later he himself revised them: 'Contrary to my previous position,' he wrote in 1979, 'some treatment programmes do have appreciable effect on recidivism . . . New evidence from our current study leads me to reject my original conclusion . . . I have hesitated up to now, but the evidence in our survey is simply too overwhelming to ignore.' The word 'treatment' was itself ambiguous: formerly it had implied the 'medical model', in which the offender was seen as 'maladjusted' and needed to be diagnosed and 'cured'; now it was becoming more like a contract, in which the offender was encouraged to identify his own problems and agreed to accept help in overcoming them.

But the damage had been done. Especially in prisons, people drew the wrong conclusions. The rehabilitative ideology was no longer fashionable, and it fell into desuetude. The Home Office brown book, *Prisons and the Prisoner* (1977), supported the dispiriting approach of 'humane containment', to be endorsed by the May Committee on

Prisons in 1979. They might have said, 'The treatment offered in prisons is inadequate and is counteracted by the harmful effects of imprisonment itself, therefore we must improve the treatment and offer it outside prison whenever possible.' Instead they said, 'Nothing works anyway, so we may as well give up trying and restrict ourselves to "humane containment" as an end in itself.' Rule number one of the Prison Rules, 1964, though a pious hope, was at least idealistic: 'The purpose of the training and treatment of convicted prisoners shall be to encourage and assist them to lead a good and useful life.' In practice, this was superceded by a more negative approach known as 'positive custody' – 'The purpose of the detention of convicted prisoners shall be to keep them in custody' – with preparation for discharge last on the list of objectives (Committee of Inquiry 1979, para 4.26).

This uninspired, even nihilist, approach was not helped by an administrative change in the mid-1960s. For nearly a century – from 1878 onward – the prisons had been managed by the Prison Commission, and for 40 years it, and especially its successive chairmen, had a tradition of adopting liberal principles and defending them against the outcry when anything went wrong. In 1963, however, the Prison Commission was absorbed into the Home Office. The motive was good; the effect, bad. It was considered necessary to bring the custodial and non-custodial parts of the system under one roof – probation had from its inception been handled within the Home Office. The sensible move would have been to redefine the Prison Commission's role so as to include the non-custodial side. In the Home Office a different tradition prevailed: the Minister must be protected from embarrassment. Formerly, it was said, a prison governor could do anything that was not forbidden; now he can do nothing unless he had permission. To make matters worse, in 1966 George Blake escaped from Wormwood Scrubs. The laxity in preventing escapes from custody caught up with the prison service; so lax was it indeed that the prison administration had no photograph of Blake on file so as to alert police forces, the media and the public. The response was predictable. In his report on the matter, Lord (Louis) Mountbatten recommended stricter security measures, most of which were brought in, and humane ones to reduce the pressures to escape, most of which were not. He also recommended a single fortress prison for those whose escape would present a major danger to the public or embarrassment to the government; but concentration of such prisoners in one prison was rejected in favour of dispersal, which has not been a resounding success. The official reaction to Mountbatten was retrogressive. The emphasis on security put the prospect of penal progress back 20 years.

Sentencing: chasing the chimera

As the new subject of criminology was developed during the 1960s, after the establishment of the Institute of Criminology at Cambridge, criminologists began to look at a new aspect of the law enforcement progress: sentencing. In 1969 Dr Nigel Walker, of Nuffield College, Oxford (later professor of criminology and director of the Institute of Criminology at Cambridge), published *Sentencing in a Rational Society*; a year later Dr David Thomas, at Cambridge, produced *Principles of Sentencing*. They sought to elucidate the principles followed by courts when passing judgment. First, Nigel Walker identified several aims present in the process of deciding a sentence. Some were practical, such as to reduce crime by deterrence or rehabilitation; others symbolic, such as retribution against the offender and denunciation of the offence. Then David Thomas examined the decisions of the Court of Appeal (Criminal Division), focusing more specifically on the types and lengths of sentences and the reasons given. Unfortunately he undertook his study at a time when a practice of imposing long sentences had already grown up. He identified two main types of sentence, the 'individualized', or 'rehabilitative', and the 'tariff', or 'deterrent'. The courts, like M. Jourdain speaking prose, discovered that they had method and principles all along. The judges avidly imbibed Dr Thomas's work as standardizing their erratic sentencing policy and practices. As one man commented, after being sentenced to seven years' imprisonment for a not very serious indecent assault, 'Some people are mighty careless about other people's time.' The trouble was that the appeal court judges saw only the alleged excesses of the

51

sentencing courts and set about correcting them (if at all) on the basis of a biased sample.

But even then the picture was not as clear as that. Courts were not always sure which principle they were applying: Borstal, for example, might be 'deterrent' because it was custodial, or 'rehabilitative' because it provided training. (In fact, in the period of gross overcrowding in the late 1960s, the average period in Borstals had fallen from about 18 months to eight – and training was available only for part of that time.) The punitive purposes, such as deterrence and retribution, were assumed to be more or less the same, but in fact they were based on different principles. A retributive sentence reflected the seriousness of the offence, regardless of its effect on the offender; a deterrent one was exactly the opposite – a murderer might need no deterrent other than the conviction itself to prevent him from repeating his offence, while, as we have seen, the prospect of many years of penal servitude can be insufficient to deter a hungry woman from stealing food.

The edifice of sentencing is erected on at least two fondly held judicial shibboleths: (a) that sentences have a significant and positive impact on the volume of crime, as courts, politicians, and the media profess to believe; and (b) that the sentencing structure combining all these purposes is consistent and produces an equal distribution of fairness among offenders.

It is worth looking briefly at the ostensible purposes of sentencing, as identified by these scholars. The main one is a utilitarian one: crime reduction. It is supposed to be achieved by four main methods – individual deterrence, general deterrence, rehabilitation, and containment. Let us consider these in turn.

The first method is intended to deter the individual offender from re-offending. Apart from the fact that people protest vehemently that they will not be caught next time, the problem here is that it is hard to impose methods that are sufficiently frightening, without also being barbaric. If we were to countenance cutting off the hands of thieves, it might possibly prevent the handless and helpless from thieving again. Even socially tolerable sanctions serve only to incapacitate a person for law-abiding life and often make him more inclined to avenge himself on society than to conform to its wishes. Punishment makes people think of themselves, rarely of their victims, or society.

Second, deterrent sentencing is supposed to deter other potential offenders. This was the principle on which Admiral George Byng was shot, according to Voltaire's sardonic remark: 'Dans ce pays-ci il est bon de tuer de temps en temps un amiral pour encourager les autres' (In this country it is thought desirable to kill an admiral from time to time to encourage the others [*Candide*, chap 23]). Here more than anywhere there is an ethical problem which is usually skirted round. There are strong arguments for saying that to inflict harm on anyone with the intention of influencing other people cannot be ethically or socially justified. As Lord Justice Asquith said, all exemplary punishments are unjust, and they are unjust to precisely the extent that they are exemplary. Even if the principle were accepted as a necessary evil, it could be acceptable only if it could be shown to work. But there is no conclusive evidence, except for some further examples of anecdotal penology, or at least impressionistic evidence so fondly exhibited by judges. Thirty years ago, for example, after an outbreak of attacks on black people in Notting Hill, nine youths were sentenced to four years' imprisonment (at least double the normal sentence). The judge, Mr Justice (later Lord) Salmon, made a firm condemnation of racial harassment – which was fine, but piling on the agony of extended incarceration was wholly unnecessary. The attacks stopped, and the sentences were given the credit. But investigation by researchers has shown that other factors, such as increased police activity, were just as likely to have been responsible. If anything, it is the probability of being caught that makes the best deterrent: an old truism, but supported by modern research. The trouble is that the detection rate for most crimes is depressingly low – hence the lack of deterrent effect.

Deterrents can indeed have side effects that are counter-productive. Once a crime has been committed, the more severe the penalty, the more a person is under pressure to threaten witnesses, including the victim, in order to escape conviction. Conversely, in cases such as child abuse, the prospect of seeing a father (for example) sent to prison for a long time may make the victim feel not only more afraid but also more guilty at the prospect of reporting him. The burden of proof should be on the courts to show that punishment, especially imprisonment, is in the public interest. It might help if probation officers, too, presented their recommendations in terms of the public interest. This would still, in the great majority of cases, lead them to recommend non-custodial sanctions – but with a better chance that these would be acceptable to the courts. The basic problem about deterrence is that it proceeds upon the assumption that offenders calculate cause and effect before engaging in the criminal act. The fact is that most offenders – at least those who land up in prison – have a sense of their own immunity, or even, like gamblers, enjoy the risk, and pay little regard to the consequences of their acts.

The subject is in any event very complex, but perhaps these few points will be enough to persuade the legislators and popular press that increasing penalties is not necessarily the best way to counter crimes, however unpleasant; indeed if we put our faith in quack remedies, it may divert us from the search for more effective ones – to say nothing of better preventive policies.

The third practical objective of sentencing is to rehabilitate the offender. The efficacy of 'rehabilitative' sentences is at least open to question, as we have seen, even if some critics have been unduly dismissive. Often the educative measures have not been given the resources they need, or have been conducted in prison, which outweighs their beneficial effects; or the research itself has been inadequately designed, but that does not necessarily mean that the claims of the project itself are invalid. Some 'rehabilitative' sentences, particularly those based on indeterminate duration or compulsory treatment, can be more restrictive than punitive ones. A further problem with the rehabilitative sentence is that it does not appear to hold the offender responsible for his actions; by appearing to see the causes of his offence in his psychological make-up or his social surroundings, it fails to symbolize the fact that he did wrong and, in many cases, a victim suffered.

Fourth, it is often argued, even if offenders are neither deterred nor rehabilitated, at least they can be contained. There are some offenders for whom this is inevitable, if they pose an intolerable danger to others. But at the other end of the scale there are many whose offences do not justify a severe sentence; imprisoning them is as likely as not to increase the chances that they will re-offend, and given the low rate of detection, particularly of petty crimes, imprisoning for a few weeks or months the small number who are caught is not going to have any significant effect on the total volume of crime.

The argument here is not that no one is ever deterred by the prospect of punishment, nor that prisons do not contain some people who would otherwise be outside committing crimes; it is that, except in the most serious cases, any such effects are liable to be heavily outweighed by the damaging effects of imprisonment; worse than that, if society puts its trust in a method of crime control which is ineffective or even counterproductive, it is actually endangering its citizens through complacency. For those with long memories, one might say that prisons are to crime as the Maginot Line was to the invasion of France: the fortifications were impregnable, but the German army in 1940 bypassed them with consummate ease, to the discomfiture of the Allied commanders.

But even if imprisonment, and punishments generally, achieve no tangible results at all, there is still another possible justification: retribution. The first thing to say about this is that current practice is unjust: imprisonment is the most serious punishment in the land, yet many people are in prison for what are by any standards minor offences. But leaving that aside, various justifications are offered for retributive sentencing. It can be seen as cancelling out the advantage gained by the offender through the crime. But most important, it symbolizes the fact that the offender's behaviour is not tolerated. Professor Walker has called this function 'denunciation'. When there is an outcry against a particular sentence because it is too 'lenient', what it means is that it is considered to be less than sentences imposed on other offenders who have committed crimes of comparable gravity. Alternatively, people compare the harm done to the victim with the impact of the sentence on the offender: a young woman may have been crippled, or even killed, for example, by a drunken driver, who is only fined, or is only disqualified from driving, or only receives a short prison sentence, which may even be suspended. Part of the trouble here is that the law and its penalties are based on the state of mind of the offender, rather than on the harm inflicted on the victim: to drive while drunk is only reckless or negligent, and there was no deliberate intent to kill or injure that person. This was the basis for Barbara Wootton's (1963) compelling assault on the lawyers' adherence to *mens rea*: society's interest is in the harm inflicted on the victim, and the offender's motive or intention is relevant only to the disposal on conviction. This could be overcome if the scales of justice were balanced using a different system of weighting: rather than attempt the impossible calculation involved in making the offender endure an amount of suffering proportionate to his guilty intentions, he would be required to cancel out his crime, even if only symbolically, by reparative acts, or payments, proportionate to the harm caused to the victim or to the community.

With such disparate aims in sentencing policy and practice, it is not surprising that there is inconsistency. The common mistake is to assume that this is due to the human fallibility of judges and magistrates; that if only they had better training, or detailed guidelines, or stricter legislative constraints, something like a fair and effective sentencing policy could be devised. Here we should acquit the judges. The reason why it is not achieved is that it is unachievable. It is almost inevitable that a sentence, adequate on retributive grounds, will be too light or too heavy on deterrent grounds, too short or too long for purposes of rehabilitation, and so on. To attempt to balance the aims against each other is to ensure that none of them is attained. It is essential to decide which of the objectives is to take precedence, if there is a clash. This has in effect been done in those states of America which have adopted sentencing guidelines – and we are in the process of disastrously initiating them. Reacting against both the indeterminate sentence and the inconsistency of courts, these states have decreed that sentencing should be based on a tabulation: a certain category of offence must lead to a certain penalty. One of the best-known schemes of this kind is in Minnesota. A sentencing commission has been established; this insulates policy from the legislature, which does, however, have the last word. The commission has drawn up a table, in which the columns represent the number of the offender's previous convictions and the horizontal rows indicate the category of offence. Each box in the table contains a main number, which represents the length of the sentence in months, with a lower and a higher number, indicating the differences to be allowed for mitigating or aggravating circumstances. This does not, however, completely tie down the judges; judges may depart from the guidelines if they give reasons. If there is a public demand for a change in the sentence for a particular offence, referral to the commission provides a pause to ensure that this will not introduce inconsistencies in relation to other sentences. The entire scale of sentences, more or less consistent in relation to each other, is adjusted downward if the prisons become full: not exactly a principled basis for sentencing but a practical and economical one. The Criminal Justice Act 2003 provides an astounding example. If a person is convicted of a 'normal' murder, the starting point of the tariff is 15 years. If racism is an aggravating factor in the homicidal event, the starting point is 30 years. What sort of calculus can produce such a result?!

What this amounts to is that the adoption of sentencing guidelines cuts through the ambiguities and puts one principle of sentencing in the first place: punishment. The question can then be posed to legislators and electors: do you recognize that what you are doing, at great financial and human cost, is simply inflicting further pain on the offender and his family (in addition to what he has already caused to the victim) because you have admitted the reality that any attempt to rehabilitate offenders has been subordinated to retribution? If what is most important is to symbolize society's condemnation of wrongdoing, is there not a constructive method of doing so? There is a good case for saying that the principle with the fewest objections is the reparative goal: this does not prevent the others being present as desirable side effects. There is, however, a danger: if reparation were *added* to the list of aims, without being adopted as the *primary* goal, this would add to the confusion. The introduction of the Sentencing Advisory Panel and, later, the Sentencing Council, adopts this problem. As in the United States, the effect paradoxically is to ratchet up the lengths of prison sentences.

Changing the practice in a penal society

The 1960s ended with two very problematic innovations in the criminal justice system of this country: parole and suspended sentences; the 1970s began with some developments of great potential significance. They had their origins in the introduction, in 1964, of *ex gratia* state compensation for victims of violent crime (later to be put on a statutory footing), and in two reports by the Advisory Council on the Penal System, in 1970: *Non-custodial and Semi-custodial Penalties* (chaired by Baroness Wootton) and *Reparation by the Offender* (chaired by Lord Justice, later Lord Chief Justice, Widgery).

One suggestion, put forward at a Howard League conference in 1970, was for a requirement to attend a day training centre (the more general term is now 'day centre'), in the context of a probation order. Although the Wootton report did not give as much prominence to this idea as to the community service order, the centres were introduced in the Act of 1972, which was amended in 1982. This may not seem a major innovation, but it is significant for two reasons. One is that day centres have provided a focus for a change in the definition of 'rehabilitation'; this was regarded less and less as a form of diagnosis and treatment for 'maladjusted' or otherwise deviant offender-patients, and more as offering offender-clients themselves an opportunity to define the difficulties they face and helping them to devise programmes toward overcoming them. Second, a day centre can provide continuity for probation initiatives, such as literary programmes, social skills training, groups for sexual offenders, and so on, which otherwise tend to fade out when the individual probation officers who started them leave the area. Day centres now exist in almost all probation areas, though not in all districts; they can provide courts with a useful sanction when probation officers recognize that imprisonment would be worse than useless but feel that something more specific than a standard probation order and supervision is required.

The main recommendation of the Wootton Committee was the community service order, included in the same Act. This is probably the most significant innovation in the theory and practice of criminal justice for at least half a century. In essence it is a way of giving effect to the basic principle that a person harms the community by his offence and should therefore make amends by doing something beneficial for the community. But there is more to it than that. The intention is that the offender should use any skills or qualities he possesses for the common good, rather than merely endure the mind-crippling boredom which is a dominant feature of present-day prison life. Those who complain that community service is not unpleasant enough are wide of the mark, because the objective is reparation by the offender, not punishment of the offender. There is a possibility of enabling him to build himself up into a good citizen, rather than portraying him as an outcast. As far as possible his task in the community will be related to his abilities rather than to his offence. To encourage this approach, the courts have been given the power only to order community service, not to specify the type; that is done by the probation service, usually after discussion with the offender. This prevents the courts from imposing tasks that are ill-suited to the individual offender, or fanciful or punitive. The Advisory Council recommended that, wherever possible, offenders should work either with beneficiaries in person or alongside volunteers; this avoids a basic criticism of prisons – that they herd together those who have nothing in common except their criminality – and offers the hope that the offender may pick up different attitudes from those of his usual associates. To avoid the charge that this would be a form of forced labour, which is forbidden under international conventions, the imposition of a community service order depends on the consent of the offender – not an entirely free consent, it is true, because in many cases the alternative would be a custodial sentence; but it does mean that community service can be avoided by anyone who is very reluctant to undertake it.

There have been problems with community service, practical and theoretical. The practical ones have been mainly associated with finding enough tasks of the right kind. This can be time-consuming, and some probation areas have had to limit the number of community service orders they can recommend to the courts – an injustice to the offender, if imprisonment was not necessary, and a false economy if ever there was one, given the much higher cost of imprisonment. Community service orders are for a maximum of 240 hours, taking up a year to complete; this means that they are not considered suitable for very serious offences. The work must be of a kind which would not otherwise be done by employees earning their livelihood. To ensure this, representatives of trade unions have been closely associated with community service from the start, although in fact a number of tasks such as decorating the homes of old people have been allowed. Voluntary organizations do not always find it easy to provide or supervise tasks, especially if the person is available only at weekends. Travel can be a problem, particularly in rural areas. As a result, some community service organizers have resorted to what is deprecatingly called a 'chain-gang' approach. The offenders are put into groups and given manual work with no contact with beneficiaries or other members of the public. On paper this makes supervision more economical, but in practice it is difficult for the supervisor to exercise control in those circumstances. Some tasks are not of benefit to sections of the public most in need: some people might regard clearing canals as conservation, for example, but to the offenders it may seem like working for 'bloody boat owners'.

Nevertheless a large number of imaginative tasks has been found, and a high proportion has been completed satisfactorily. A few examples include work for homeless people, one-to-one placements helping handicapped children to read or to swim, working with police cadets on a conservation project, running a coffee bar in a courthouse, providing transport for old people, taking disabled people shopping. Some of these, such as the last-mentioned, combine group placements with direct contact with beneficiaries.

A more fundamental problem with community service orders, however, has been the confusion of aims which appears to be endemic in criminal justice. In an effort to make the new measure acceptable to all shades of opinion, the Advisory Council wrote:

> The proposition that some offenders should be required to undertake community service should appeal to different varieties of penal philosophy. To some, it would be simply a more constructive and cheaper alternative to imprisonment; by others it would be seen as introducing into the penal system a new dimension with an emphasis on reparation to the community; others again would regard it as giving effect to the old adage that the punishment should fit the crime; while still others would stress the value of bringing offenders into close touch with those members of the community who are most in need of help and support.

It might change the offenders' outlook and be seen by them as 'not wholly negative and punitive', and they might gain from 'the wholesome influence of those who choose voluntarily to engage in those tasks'. Thus the advantages claimed included punishment, rehabilitation, avoidance of imprisonment, and reparation. Inevitably, these goals proved incompatible; predictably, different courts, probation officers, and supervisors put them in different orders of priority. This causes not only inconsistency but also injustice. In one court an offender who in no way deserves imprisonment may be given a community service order because it is thought to be beneficial to him; but if he re-offends and appears before another court, which regards community service as the 'last chance' before imprisonment, it will regard him as having had that last chance (although that was not the intention of the previous court) and send him to prison.

There is evidence that a majority of the public, including victims of crime, favour the idea of community service by offenders, and that offenders themselves generally feel that it is a fair sanction, which is important in terms of promoting respect for the law. It seems, therefore, that community service is worth retaining. But if we accept that one aim of any sanction should have priority, for the sake of consistency and justice, which should it be? It is no surprise to find that the utilitarian goal of reducing crime is probably not achieved better by community service orders than by any other sanction. About half of offenders are reconvicted within two years of the imposition of the order, which is comparable to the proportion reconvicted within two years of release from custody. It is clearly not a punishment, since it can succeed even when offenders enjoy it – some even continue their tasks voluntarily afterwards. It does not seem to have helped the system by reducing the prison population: not only the number but the *proportion* of convicted offenders has risen since community service came into effect in 1973, whereas the decrease has been in the proportion of offenders fined. The other aim is reparation, and here community service orders have been among the most successful sanctions: about three-quarters of offenders complete the required number of hours of reparation, and most of the remainder complete at least some hours. Reparation to the community, then, is a largely achievable goal and is largely accepted by the community.

A third development at the beginning of the 1970s was the return of reparation as a sanction. The desirability of leaving the victim to pursue a remedy in the civil court would seldom be worthwhile, even if 'nil contribution legal aid' were available to the victim as claimant, or if the State undertook the proceedings on the victim's behalf. It was suggested that the whole matter should be dealt with at one hearing, in the criminal court, and that the victim should not be required to apply to the court, as had been the case since the Probation of Offenders Act of 1907. The result was a considerable increase in the number of compensation orders made, particularly for property offences, although in cases of violence, compensation orders are much less common, purely because the offenders are most likely to be sent to prison, where they have almost no opportunity to make reparation. Reparation can be regarded as an improvement in principle: the victim receives some compensation, the offender is required to pay it. In practice it has not worked quite so well. Some victims did not really want compensation, especially if it was to arrive in irregular driblets for several months, reminding them of an experience they would rather forget; but they were not asked. There was no procedure for agreeing on the amount of the compensation; the Court of Appeal decided that if this raised complicated or contentious questions, the criminal court was not the place to resolve them. Little attention is paid to the *presentation*, to the symbolic effect of compensation. The victim receives a cheque from the court, with a form giving bare details; the offender, similarly, has to pay compensation to the court in exactly the same way as he pays a fine, and there is no procedure for reminding him that compensation is not merely a different form of penalty paid to the State but a repayment to the person whom he wronged by his act.

Ten years later the Criminal Justice Act of 1982 took the process further. It provided that where the offender is not in a position to pay both a fine and compensation, the latter takes precedence, and that a compensation order can be made in its own right, unaccompanied by a penalty. This is potentially of great significance, implying as it does that society's response to a crime can take the form of compensation to the victim rather than punishment by the State;

but it has not had as great an impact as it might, because courts have tended to look on compensation as a form of punishment, rather than as an alternative to punishment. Thus they are denying to both victims and offenders the feeling that amends have been made. Nevertheless the restorative principle is now firmly on the statute book, and it may be predicted that it will have a place in future sentencing textbooks. It is to be hoped that the procedure will be revised so as to place more emphasis on the reparative purpose, rather than the retributive.

An even more significant step toward reparation stemmed from the report of a Howard League Working Party, *Profits of Crime*, following the law's failure to secure forfeiture of the ill-gotten gains of the drug smugglers caught by 'Operation Julie'. This report outlined a method of seizing ill-gotten gains of crime and freezing them in bank accounts before, or at the time of, the offender's arrest. The court of conviction would then have assets readily available for confiscation by the State. The principle was adopted in relation to drug offenders in the Drug Trafficking Offences Act of 1986 and has been extended to all serious fraud cases.

Other developments were taking place in the 1970s which had not yet come to prominence. One was the Victims Support Scheme, originated in Bristol in 1974. The principle is very simple: volunteers contact people who have been victims of crime to see whether they can offer support or practical help. But, as with reparation, the implications are considerable: the criminal justice system cannot be regarded as complete unless it takes account of the victim. At about the same time, in North America, this was being recognized in another way: where victim and offender knew each other, they were invited to try to resolve their differences before mediators, rather than through the criminal courts. Later the principle was extended to crimes by strangers. There is considerable interest in these ideas in this country; experimental projects have been funded by the Home Office, and a Forum for Initiatives in Reparation and Mediation (FIRM) has been established to spread the idea and promote good standards.

Sentencing: another try

Later in the 1970s a new attempt to reform sentencing was made by the Advisory Council on the Penal System. It was prompted, once again, by the desire to reduce the excessive use of imprisonment (for the sake of the prison system as well as of offenders); but the Council took the opportunity to try to introduce some consistency. This was not a re-think of the underlying principles, such as has been considered in the foregoing discussion; it started from the undeniable premise that maximum penalties have been fixed by Parliament during the past 100 years without any coherent basis to them. The arbitrary starting point, as we have seen, was the biblical number seven, which had been used in the days of transportation. Over the years the judges had been conscious of the inconsistencies and had done their best to iron them out through the notional construction of the informal tariff. For that reason the Advisory Council took as its starting point, in proposing a revision of statutory maxima, the sentences actually imposed by the courts; there was another, more pragmatic, reason – namely, that if the principles were based on the judges' own practice, it would not be possible for critics to say that an extraneous body of people was claiming to know better than the courts.

The pressure on prison accommodation was becoming so great that the Advisory Council had issued an interim report in 1976 urging a reduction in the use of imprisonment; it had a marginal impact, but only for a year or two, after which sentence lengths reverted to form. In its final report, *Sentences of Imprisonment: A Review of Maximum Penalties*, published in 1978, it attempted to combine consistency with a gentle downward thrust, by setting the 'normal maxima' at the level below which 90 per cent of current sentences fell. Courts would not lose their discretion to impose longer sentences if they felt it necessary to protect the public: the 'normal maxima' could be exceeded under certain stringent conditions and with appropriate safeguards. Unlike previous proposals of the Advisory Council, however, these were not to be adopted. They received no ministerial approbation and have lain fallow in the fields of officialdom. They might just get a revival in the newly created Ministry of Justice. From one side they were attacked as giving courts too much power, because it was suggested that if the 'normal maximum' was exceeded, according to strict rules defining dangerousness, no further maximum would be prescribed. It was also attacked by academic criminologists for introducing a system of 'bifur-cation' of sentences, separating out the ordinary offender from the exceptional, dangerous one on predictive grounds.

But from the other flank, the popular press succeeded in making the proposals politically unacceptable; ignoring the word 'normal', they presented the scheme as meaning that, for example, the maximum penalty for rape would be seven years. The headline writer in the *Daily Mail*, quite irre-sponsibly, called it a 'Rapists' Charter'. Sensible public debate was rendered impotent, and there could be no rational discussion, except in academic circles. With hind-sight, it may be that the fundamental flaw was for the Advisory Council to suppose that imprisonment could, or should, be a yardstick by which society's response to criminal conduct would be meted out. It had proceeded upon the retention of the sentencing structure as reflected in practice. That may be a clue to the search for a sounder principle for upholding the law.

Conclusion

The efforts during the post-war years brought little for society's comfort. There has been an unceasing silting up of the prisons and thus an increasing reliance on a scarce and costly resource. The prison system lurches from crisis to crisis, unrelieved by the imposition of a sound penal policy. Much, but not all that much, has been achieved to mitigate the worst effects of more and longer terms of imprisonment. Whatever may be said against parole, without it the crisis in the prison population would have been even more chronic. Non-custodial penalties have undoubtedly been on the whole beneficial. But they have only nibbled at the edges of a system at heart socially unhealthy and unproductive, without resolving the contradictions in its philosophy. Nothing in the last 30 years has arrested the inherited penal philosophy. Yet the prison system needs to be turned inside out.

Chapter 3

Depopulating the Prisons: Escaping the Trap

Prisons exist because societies have found it expedient from time to time to provide places in which to segregate some of their citizenry from social intercourse. Originally these were not designed to be punitive; not unknown before the rapid growth in population in the nineteenth century, but intensified by it, imprisonment has over the years been variously used more or less to satisfy fluctuating purposes – punishment (retribution, the so-called 'justice model'), deterrence (general and individual), rehabilitation (reform), humane containment, or social defence. These several purposes have vied with one another for pre-eminence; none of them has attained such a status; instead they have intermingled profitlessly and even harmfully. A simple, unconfused, minimalist use of imprisonment, in order to justify the interference in human liberty by a modern industrialized society in response to certain kinds of social problems, has barely been argued for, although there has at times been a movement for reduction in the prison population. Reductionism has an appeal to the moderate mind. Minimalism attracts the radical thinker.

75

Given this state of flux, the proper function (whatever it be) of imprisonment as a major response to crime cannot be regarded as either static or immutable. Whereas in the nineteenth century imprisonment was regarded as the ordinary consequence of a conviction for a range of serious or repeated offences – and often for trivial ones too – the twentieth century has seen society's repertoire of sanctions enlarged, to soften the iron equation between crime and punishment. Prison remains, however, the core of the contemporary penal system. The proposal for change must be to make non-custodial sanctions the normal response to all crimes, with prison as a resort where dangerousness alone positively dictates containment, or where a period of temporary removal from society is absolutely necessary, and not merely justifiable, to sustain or support a programme of social re-education in the community. This fundamental change must be judged in the context of the criminal process, which itself faces a crisis.

Criminal justice as operated today presents a two-fold problem. First, it is failing to be fair, humane and effective. It is not fair because sentences are inconsistent, many people are in prison for minor offences, others sent to prison for too long, and the prison disciplinary system is in need of major reform – to name but a few injustices. To say that our prisons are inhumane is a cliché – not only in the notoriously overcrowded local prisons, with their degrading squalor and enforced idleness, but in the longer-term, high-security prisons, with their restrictions on correspondence and visits and their isolated locations, which could hardly be better designed to break any family ties which the offender may have had before his sentence. The operation of the parole system and repressive security procedures are an extra burden for long-term prisoners. The ineffectiveness of the machinery of justice is also clear, both from the number of crimes committed and the numbers who re-offend after being dealt with by the system. So much is generally acknowledged.

But there is a second, largely unacknowledged problem. This lies in the fact that the criminal justice system, as at present constructed, is not even *capable* of being fair, humane and effective. The criminal process cannot be fair so long as there are differing objectives with no agreement as to which of them is given priority. To punish some while attempting to rehabilitate others is bound to lead to anomalies. Only a minority of offenders are caught; to add to their punishment in the uncertain hope of frightening others over whom they have no control and whom, for the most part, they do not know, would be unfair even if it worked, and is indefensible when it doesn't. In the nineteenth century, the prison administrator du Cane saw that there was no logical basis for matching an amount of culpability with a period of time in prison; there still isn't. Terms of imprisonment cannot be measured against any rational calculus.

Humanity and punishment are at loggerheads. The more punitive, the less humane, and vice versa. Any punishment that is at all severe, moreover, is bound to inflict hardship on the offender's family, if he or she has one.

In a similar way, fairness and effectiveness also conflict. Even if it were possible to prescribe how long the punishment or compulsory treatment of a particular individual would need to be in order to be effective, this would bear no relation to the seriousness of his offence. Experience shows, too, that insofar as punishment is effective in changing behaviour, it does so only under specific conditions: it must be certain, inflicted soon after the prohibited behaviour, reinforced at intervals, and combined with a proper opportunity and incentive to behave in a different way. The criminal justice system is deficient in all these respects. Conversely, it has been shown that the effects of rewards on behaviour are much more long-lasting, even if the rewards are intermittent; they need not be tangible but include the opportunity to gain self-respect and the respect of others and a reasonably satisfying life. This is not a panacea to abolish selfish behaviour: many people who apparently have every advantage in life still turn to crime. But the majority of offenders who are caught by the criminal justice agencies, and who cause the most fear, are the have-nots who have little inclination to conform and have experienced educational failure and social rejection. For them the incentives to conform are weak. In our society we are all bombarded by propaganda which constantly hammers home the philosophy that status and happiness depend upon the possession of money and goods, but many young men and women have poor prospects of acquiring much of either through socially acceptable means. Any process of law which makes them feel further rejected can only exacerbate the problems it seeks to solve. This is not a plea for softness, but for insight and realism. The starting point for reducing crime, therefore, should be the rewards of doing right rather than the fear of the consequences of wrongdoing: not *criminal* justice but *social* justice achievable outside the criminal justice system, and that means applying rewards as well as dis-rewards.

Defining the goals

Attitudes to criminal justice, as well as to imprisonment, are trapped under the accumulated weight of tradition. This is compounded by an element of conviction penology, a reluctance either to question assumptions or to base policy on research. In the first flush of the twenty-first century, we shall be well advised to start with a clean slate – and nowadays if you stand outside a prison, you will not have to wait long before a prisoner climbs on the roof and throws one down to you.

The first requirement of the framers of any rational penal policy is to try to define the aims of society in regard to anti-social behaviour. As a starting point, four in descending order of priority could be suggested:

- To try to reduce the level of crime in which people harm each other (crime reduction).
- To show a prime concern for the victims of crime, and as far as possible restore them to their previous condition (victims' support).
- To show offenders and others that lawbreaking is not tolerated (denunciation) by involving them in community services.
- To contain the few from whom society can be protected in no other way (residual imprisonment) in much the same way as they are kept out of circulation through the mental health system.

Reduction of crime

Crime prevention policy has to be both specific and general. At a specific level, ordinary precautions are still needed; the increasing anonymity and mobility of modern society, particularly in large cities, means that locks, streetlights and other security measures will continue to be necessary for the foreseeable future. But it is important not to rely on them entirely, nor to become preoccupied with them. In that case people would be fearful to walk in the streets, which in turn would become deserted and dangerous. The Englishman's home would not be an accessible castle but an impregnable citadel; that would be intolerable.

Crime prevention should also involve the community.

Neighbourhood Watch, so long as it does not become a forum for vigilantes, may be part of the solution; schemes of this kind not only use the local community but also help, with police assistance, to build it up when it is withering away. Often, something more active is needed; it may require the help of a catalyst from outside. Numerous schemes have been promoted, by NACRO among others (which, although its name is the National Association for the Care and Resettlement of Offenders, devotes considerable energy to crime prevention as well as to penal policy). An example among many is the Bushbury Triangle project in Wolverhampton. In 1981 the area had many empty houses, a high level of transfer requests, high crime rates, no on-site community facilities and much damage, litter and disrepair. Local agencies were brought together in a steering committee, considerable trouble was taken to consult residents, and an action plan was developed. In addition to home security improvements, there was a modernization programme and a fencing scheme (of the garden variety, not as a receptacle for stolen goods); a residents' association was established and a community centre set up in two empty houses, which residents agreed to manage. In 1985 a careful evaluation was made: it found that burglaries and vandalism of both shops and dwellings had been substantially reduced. Thus the project reduced crime and helped to recreate a sense of community.

It has to be remembered that there is no such thing as 'crime'. There are only crime*s*. Each type of criminal event has to be approached with a different preventive policy.

The prevention of offences against the Inland Revenue and the Health and Safety legislation requires measures quite different from those designed to combat sexual assaults and football hooliganism. They may have in common that some individuals are pursuing their own gratification at the expense of others; but the means of educating them to understand this, and to make it more difficult for them to offend without being detected, vary according to the nature of the specific criminal event, let alone the offence with which the lawyers label it.

A crime control strategy needs to operate at many different levels. Criminal justice is only one level, and a costly and cumbersome one at that. It has been shown, for example, that young people are more likely to engage in delinquency if parental discipline is too authoritarian, neglectful or inconsistent, and if it uses physical punishment; if children feel unwanted; or if there is violence in the family. Family problems can be tackled not by lectures from politicians but, for example, by television programmes designed to help parents understand discipline and 'positive parenting'; by providing respite services with baby-sitting or holidays for families under stress; and by crisis interveners or mediators, professionals, or volunteers brought in after the police have been called to a case of domestic violence, to offer help with problems in the hope of avoiding a recurrence. Schools can go some way toward making up for the deficiencies in the upbringing provided by children's own parents, but only if they are given the resources for the task. Challenging recreational programmes for young people are also needed; and for a society to fail to provide work for many thousands of young people is both dangerous and disgraceful. A prospect for a life of unemployment, and even unemployability, is more than any person should be asked to face. It is a recipe for a life of crime.

The essential point about a policy for persuading people not to behave badly toward one another is that it does not belong primarily in the department of criminal justice. It is a social problem and calls for a social solution. A person's behaviour is noted by the police occasionally, by other people much of the time, and by him or herself all the time. The effectiveness of social control varies proportionately; the trouble is, so does the difficulty of persuading people to exercise it. The Serious Fraud Office can, for example, police a small proportion of the activities of the major fraudsters. Other financial agencies can assist in controlling fraud. This is not to suggest, of course, that the morality of the City begins and ends with paying its bills; the increasing interest in ethical investment, avoiding companies whose stock-in-trade is damaging to life and health, suggests one way in which the morality of the finance houses could be taken further.

It is not easy to change attitudes and behaviour, but neither is it impossible; in recent years we have seen how public education can make an impact on, for example, dropping litter, environmental conservation, drinking and driving and sexual promiscuity – although needless to say there is still a long distance to go. The power of example is also important; although it is hard to show that when prominent people behave well others are inspired to follow their example, there can be little doubt that when those at the top fall short of high standards, they give everyone else an excuse to do likewise. Crime control cannot, of course, depend entirely on such lofty ideals, but without them it will be more difficult. We will devote our attention to such matters at least the more readily if we do not delude ourselves into believing the criminal process to be effective, or allow ourselves to be distracted from sensible measures by the inutility (not to say futility) of imprisonment.

This is not the place to draw up a detailed blueprint for an entire system of law enforcement, but an outline and some examples may suggest the direction in which we might hope to move in the twenty-first century. Let us consider first a case involving assault and malicious damage. Those are, under our present system, legal categories carrying specific maximum penalties. But in many cases the background is one of the neighbours or workmates having a dispute in which they end by coming to blows. No purpose is served by invoking the full weight of the criminal law; often it is difficult to determine who the aggrieved party was, and it is likely that both have put themselves in the wrong. The way to resolve such incidents is through the underlying dispute, not through reaction to a particular act which is classified as a particular criminal event. For cases of this kind a more appropriate forum would be a neighbourhood mediation centre, where both parties could meet, with trained volunteers acting as mediators. There would be no need to decide exactly what took place, nor to allocate blame; the process would be future-oriented, and the mediators would help the disputants to agree on future behaviour which both could accept.

In more serious cases, perhaps involving a theft committed by a stranger, the same procedure would be available, but if either of the parties did not wish to take part in mediation the case would have to go to court. There would also have to be a hearing, of course, if the accused did not accept blame. The court would make a compensation order if the victim wished it; if he or she did not, or if there was no individual victim, a community service order could be imposed, or the compensation would be paid to the State. The latter would be the equivalent of a fine, but would be regarded as compensating the community for the harm caused by the offence. In cases where the offender's behaviour appeared to be linked to specific problems, such as drug or alcohol addiction, illiteracy, lack of skills, or inability to control aggression, reparation could take the form of attendance at a day centre to try to overcome them. There would be no question of imprisonment.

If an offence does not merit imprisonment, neither does failure to comply with the non-custodial sanction imposed. Failure to abide by this principle, which might be thought self-evident, leads to the imprisonment of more than 20,000 fine defaulters annually in England and Wales. The first essential is to make sure that the fine is within the offender's ability to pay, by linking the amount to his income, using the day-fine principle. A fine is inappropriate where the offender's financial difficulties led to the offence, although that would not preclude at least partial restitution. Enforcement measures should be non-custodial; they could include distraint, provided that does not cause hardship to innocent members of a family. Further sanctions, some of which are available already, could include loss of civil rights, such as the right to drive a car, to be a company director, to vote, or to possess a passport. The ultimate sanction could be 'civil death' – the withdrawal of all of these rights and privileges, which would be appropriate for serious property offenders and large-scale fraudsters and other 'white-collar' criminals, in addition to swingeing financial penalties after payment of compensation (but the restrictions should not impede their ability to earn legitimately the amount necessary to pay the compensation).

In more serious cases, the compensation or community service would extend over considerably longer periods than are usual now, in order to make up for the harm done at least symbolically, even if the loss itself could never be made good. The court would make a separate decision to authorize the use of custody if required for public protection. The effect of this would be similar to being on parole: the person would live in the community but be required to notify the authorities of his address and to report regularly, and be subject to recall if these or other conditions were breached. The safeguards for placing a person in custody should be more stringent than at present. Where there appeared to be an immediate public danger, the court would order custody immediately. Just as we put a dangerous psychopath into a special hospital, so a violent sociopath should be imprisoned for so long as there is a real risk of serious repeated violence. The sole criterion for this would be public protection. Likewise, the protection of the public would determine release. Deciding when a person may safely be released can never be easy or certain; but with only one criterion, rather than three or more as in the present parole scheme, there would be an improved chance of decisions approaching fairness and consistency. The purpose of custody would be to work toward release at the earliest possible time; the number of cases in which eventual release was not possible would be extremely small.

It may be interesting to consider the effects of this approach on one type of crime which excites strong feelings: child abuse within the family (whether cruelty, neglect, or sexual or emotional abuse). The primary approach would be to provide help with whatever problems were leading to the abuse: ignorance of parenting, intolerable housing, psychosexual disorders, or other conditions. Such a response would make it easier for the victim to report the offence, without the guilt and fear associated with being responsible for a parent's imprisonment. There is evidence that abused children remain intensely loyal to their parents and are reluctant to expose them to the criminal process.

Some offenders would also be less reluctant to admit the offence. Thus in some cases, perhaps many, it would be possible to work out a plan with the offender, with supervision, treatment, the offender's removal from home, or other appropriate measures to protect the child. Only if the offender refused to comply would it be necessary to use the law at all, and even then the family would not be broken up by imprisonment, except where no other course was possible in the interests of protection of the child or other children. This would do much more for children than any proposal to increase the maximum penalty for child cruelty and neglect.

Concern for victims

A poster shows a lawyer, a social worker and a policeman and his dog chasing after an offender, while in the middle stands a bemused victim, completely ignored. This represents, without too much exaggeration, the way victims were treated until very recently. Since 1984, however, a change has begun which may indicate the direction for the future. There is a growing concern and care for the victim; this is offered by members of the local community through Victim Support Schemes, by whom that poster is issued. There is also, in more and more cases, compensation by the offender or the State. Such visible concern would become not merely a humane addition to soften the edges of the victim's burden, but an essential part of society's balanced response to crime.

Consider for a moment what happens when there is a serious accident, like the fire at King's Cross. The first response is to look after the victims; only then is effort devoted to inquiring into how it was caused, how future accidents can be avoided, and – at the end of the list – whether anyone was culpable. Concern for the victims is shown in practical ways, through first aid and hospital treatment, if required, and symbolically, by a message of sympathy or a visit from someone of suitably high status. There is an obvious difference between accidents and crimes, in that crimes are for the most part caused by someone's deliberate act (though the borderline is not sharp: some crimes result from negligence, are not culpable because of mental illness, and so on). The focusing on the action and intention of the wrongdoer appears to have distracted our attention from the needs of the victim. Perhaps it is partly because of our desire to find someone to blame. As a society we are too prone to looking for scapegoats.

The future response to crime, then, would do well to give priority to caring for the needs of victims. Victim Support Schemes, which in 2007 became a national organization, now serve most of the population of this country, and increasing numbers of them have been offering help to victims of the most serious crimes. The establishment of the national body will help to further the aim. This expression of concern is made to victims regardless of whether the offender is known. The same is true of compensation by the State to victims of crimes of violence. A further step could be to extend this concern and compensation to victims of crimes against property, at least those living in areas of high crime rates who cannot afford insurance or cannot obtain it at all. The existence of insurance favours the better-off, again disclosing an unequal distribution of social justice.

Concern should also be shown in the way victims are treated in the criminal justice process. At present the victim is, in law, no different from any other witness; he or she is often kept waiting, called to give evidence at very short notice, subjected to an ordeal in the witness box, and kept in ignorance of the progress of the case. Now that Victim Support is drawing attention to these practices, there are moves toward a more victim-centred procedure. But this is achieved by taking steps to inform the victim and provide social assistance. It must not bring the victim into the criminal justice system. The victim's voice can properly be heard by agencies of social justice; criminal justice is not the appropriate place for helping victims to cope with the personal and social consequences of criminal activity.

There is one more way in which concern can be shown to the victim: by requiring the offender to pay compensation (if the victim wishes it, of course). When there is no individual victim, community service could be seen as reparation to the community, rather than as punishment or rehabilitation. This has the advantage that it holds the offender accountable, not allowing him to escape from his problems into prison, but it does not stigmatize him more than he has already done by his own actions, and it offers him an opportunity to work toward reacceptance in the community. Often what the victim wants most is not financial reparation, but action to make it less likely that others will become victims in a similar way; in such cases the offender can make amends by undergoing a course of training, counselling, or therapy relevant to his problems. This can usually be done while on probation or in a day centre.

Denunciation of the offence

In a country which still has a monarchy and a State Opening of Parliament, to say nothing of religious observances, it is scarcely necessary to remind people of the importance of symbolism. In the administration of justice, it is as important as anywhere. The formalities of the courtroom are redolent of symbolism and need to be retained. Formal dress (but not wigs), the trappings of the law, and due deference (but not obsequiousness) to the court are all helpful symbols of the majesty of justice – although the dock is an anachronism for which we should hold no brief. But we must accordingly take care to express the right meaning and to use appropriate symbols to do so. The trouble with the rehabilitative ideal was not only that it did not work as well as some of its advocates claimed, but also that its message appeared to be: 'You are not to be held fully accountable for what you have done; it is largely because you are maladjusted or come from a deprived environment. We will try to treat your condition.' The message of punishment, in effect, is: 'Behave well, because otherwise *you* will be made to suffer (if you are caught).' Is it not more appropriate to admonish the offender and everyone else: 'Behave well, because otherwise you will hurt *other people*, whether you are caught or not; and if you are caught, you will be required to pay back'? The symbol shifts from pain inflicted *on* the offender by the impersonality of the State, to reparation made *by* the offender to his victim, and enforceable by the State. The offender becomes involved in his own penal treatment, rather than having penalties thrust upon him. Probation and deferment of sentence were quite evidently sound sanctions, as are community service orders and compensation.

With this restorative, rather than retributive, principle of justice, the symbolism of the criminal justice system can become a more potent and fair-minded one. Not only that, but an extra step can be inserted into the process of law enforcement, so as to reduce both the burden on the system and the extent of its intervention into people's lives. Many of the less serious offenders could be dealt with in the same way as the tax fraudsters, with the administrative imposition of monetary penalties and restitution. Instead of saying: 'You have offended, therefore you must go to court and be punished', the law enforcement agencies would say: 'You have offended, therefore *if you do not make proper reparation*, you will go to court.' Instead of being devalued by overuse and consequent shortcomings in the quality of justice, the courts would be held in reserve: the likelihood of a court appearance itself would be the main deterrent. If the legal process were more selectively applied, it would carry proportionately a higher degree of social obloquy on those few who were brought here. This would also have the effect of removing the present monstrous discrimination, in which a major institution of the State introduces a gross form of inequality between certain white-collar offenders (some of whom have damaged the life or health of their employees or their customers) and other lawbreakers.

Public opinion

It is a common misconception that measures of this kind would not be acceptable to a public perceived to be punitive. The evidence has repeatedly shown otherwise. People want an adequate response, but not necessarily a punitive one – and this is as true of victims as of the public at large. In a National Opinion Poll for the *Observer* newspaper in March 1983, 85 per cent thought that it was 'a good idea' to make some offenders do community service instead of being sent to prison, and 66 per cent wanted them to pay compensation to their victims; 56 per cent did not even want burglars sent to prison. Marplan, in a survey for the BBC Broadcasting Research Department, found that 93 per cent thought offenders should have to 'make good the consequences of their crime wherever possible', and 63 per cent thought that the money from fines should go to victims. Several other surveys, both here and in other countries, have pointed in a similar direction. An interesting Canadian study found that, when asked to comment on a case where a person charged with second-degree murder was found guilty of manslaughter and sentenced to 18 months' imprisonment, 80 per cent of a sample said that the sentence was too lenient; but in a second sample, given a 500-word summary of the background of the case instead of an inadequate news report, only 15 per cent thought it was too lenient, and 44 per cent thought it too harsh. Full knowledge of the homicidal event led to a reduction in punitiveness. Populism, Thomas Jefferson once wrote, is a dangerous instrument in the hands of the politician.

Residual imprisonment

Locking people up for its own sake, or for the sake of inflicting pain, would be excluded. (Let us remember that words like 'penalty' mean the infliction of pain, or at the very least unpleasantness, as Professor Nils Christie of the University of Oslo pointed out.) But penal reformers, contrary to their caricature, accept that some people have to be deprived of their liberty for the protection of others so long as there are proper procedural safeguards. The loss of liberty need not be total. If a person has shown him or herself unfit to drive a motor vehicle, or to be a director of a company, but abides by the law in other respects, permission to engage in that specific activity is withdrawn. Law enforcement is a problem, but that should not lead us to reach for an unacceptable alternative. At present this is commonly done for a fixed period; perhaps it should be done until the offender has shown that he can be trusted. Total deprivation of liberty would be held in reserve for those who have shown themselves liable to commit serious acts of violence.

Every sentence is an intervention in the offender's life and a restriction upon his leisure, if not his liberty. In almost all cases the restriction does not need to be primarily custodial. To some extent this is already recognized, since the majority of sentences consist of probation, fines, and other non-custodial measures. But the fact that these are commonly called 'alternatives to imprisonment' – in strict usage there can only be one alternative – implies that prison is somehow the norm, and anything else is not quite the real thing, or at least is an act of mercy or leniency. Many people, from penal reformers to Home Secretaries and directors-general of prisons, struggling to accommodate all those sent to prison by the courts, have urged that the dividing line should be pushed further toward non-custodial sentences. But as long as this concept persists, there is little hope of progress. It is not a push or a shove in the direction of non-custody that is required. It is a complete reversal of roles – the official response to crime would be primarily (if not exclusively) non-custodial. Custody is a device, rarely needed, to shut either away the violent much as we do in the mental health system, or to buttress the programme of sound re-education in the community. In effect, we should stand the penal system on its head.

The basic principle would be reparative; by way of enforcement, society, through its courts, would impose only one sanction, restriction on leisure time or even choice of action, and this would normally be non-custodial. Custody could be used in support of the non-custodial measure, primarily in cases of major violence, but only until it was judged that the offender could be released without unacceptable risk to the public. Thus a non-custodial sentence for a serious offence could include an element of custody, but that would be invoked only if necessary, and with due safeguards. The reason for the custody would be to protect the public, not to inflict punishment for its own sake; this limitation, and the major reduction in numbers, would overcome many of the perils endemic in a retributive prison system.

Imprisonment itself would become wholly exceptional, because prisons would contain only those who needed to be there for the protection of the public. This means that they would be composed largely of highly disturbed and difficult inmates. The few prisons that remained in use would be differently designed to express their new function. They would be small and located in centres of population, in order to facilitate visits by the prisoners' families and to provide access to community resources.

Conclusion

The starting point for this critique has been the crisis in our prisons. The shameful fact that the United Kingdom uses imprisonment more than any of our partners in the European Union is now well known. Descriptions of the squalor and inhumanity in our prisons have been repeated, literally ad nauseam. It is essential to grasp, and to persuade our elected representatives to admit, that the solution for prison overcrowding is not to build more prisons, unless it can be shown that *every* week or month of every prison sentence being served is necessary for the protection of society. This is manifestly not the case. Prisons do protect society, but only to the extent that they temporarily restrain the minority of offenders who are prone to commit acts of serious violence; but for other purposes, notably deterrence, they are at best ineffective and at worst counterproductive. It does not make sense to subject people to inhumane (or even humane) conditions or harsh sentences, especially when it is difficult for them to find accommodation and work after release; the result is to make them reluctant or even unable to obey the rules of a society which treated them so.

The cost of imprisonment is not the strongest argument against its use. If it were effective, it would be money well spent. But the prison population includes people who resort to crime because they are homeless or live in sub-human housing conditions; to provide adequate low-cost housing would cost less than the average of £65,000 which the Home Office spent on the construction of each new prison cell. That would buy a flat in London or a row of houses in the north of England. Others become criminal when they are unemployed; it would have cost much less to employ them than to imprison them at an average cost of £35,000 a year. Experience since 1945 has been that building new prisons has not relieved overcrowding, but merely increased the prison population to breaking point.

It is hard to find any informed observer of criminal justice who believes that this level of imprisonment is either necessary or desirable. The Home Affairs Committee of the House of Commons, the Expenditure Committee, the May Committee on the Prison Service, and the chief inspector of prisons, to say nothing of the 1985 United Nations Congress on Crime Prevention and the Treatment of Offenders, are all among those who in the past have recommended reducing the prison population. Yet the official response is at best resoundingly muted, and at worst obdurate in its deafness.

Home Office Ministers (Justice Ministers since June 2007) have had a habit of stating that they are obliged to follow the wishes of the courts and that it would be wrong to 'interfere'. But this applies only to individual cases and not to the generality of offenders; the range of sanctions available, and the maximum intervention for specific offences, are rightly decided by Parliament. But every time Ministers commit themselves to building more prisons, while restricting the amount of money spent on constructive sanctions in the community, they are influencing policy by their allocation of resources. It is in a way unfortunate that probation hostels, day centres and community service programmes do not allow overcrowding; when their places are full, courts have to find an alternative, and often it is a custodial one. It should therefore be a requirement that no prison should be built or enlarged until there are enough places available in non-custodial projects to meet all needs.

In the blueprint of a rational penal policy we should reverse the trend of expansionism in prison building, start to disgorge, by stages as part of a plan of a) no expansion and b) reduction to 50,000 within ten years, large numbers of prisoners, and begin to dismantle most of our prisons, beginning with the most remote. For too long we have drifted along, entrapped in a system that simply perpetuated the use of imprisonment as the primary, appropriate response to serious (and some less than serious) unacceptable social behaviour. Imprisonment has persistently imposed a penalty (whether deserved or not) upon the many offenders sent inside by a flawed criminal justice system. But as a society we have inflicted an even greater penalty on ourselves. A rational and compassionate society incarcerates only those of its citizenry who literally cannot be safely and conveniently accommodated by, and within, the communities which spawned and nurtured their own delinquents. For any other purpose, prisons are, to quote from my text, taken from the Book of Common Prayer, 'worthy to be cut away, and clean rejected . . . some abolished and some retained.'

Chapter 4

Toughening Up the Trap

Far from escaping the trap of continued devotion to the use of imprisonment, successive administrations since 1979 – Thatcher, Major and Blair – have done nothing to stem the tide of imprisoning offenders. By the last decade of the twentieth-century criminal justice – repetitive legislative indulgencies in tinkering with sentencing policy and practice and, more importantly, addictive political opportunism, manifested by an instant over-reaction to public opinion in the tabloid media – had become inimical to rational penal thinking. To this day it remains, depressingly so. By contrast, the Prison Service, faced with the prison disturbances of 1990, more or less persistent overcrowding, and at times turbulent industrial relations, managed to function with regimes that passed penological muster under constant pressure from active penal reform groups. The prison estate (of 139 penal institutions) is intact, if fragile and vulnerable to legal challenge in respect of less than human conditions of custody. The impact of the Human Rights Act 1989 has yet to be felt in terms of compliance with the obligation to avoid inhuman and degrading treatment or punishment. Meanwhile the prison system teeters on the brink of collapse, way beyond the crisis of recent years.

The penal optimism of the 1960s, both in officialdom and among non-governmental organizations, resurfaced fleetingly in 1980. Two judgments by the majestic Lord Chief Justice, Lord Lane, had declared unequivocally sentencers' restraint in the use of custody; and where imprisonment was inevitable to reflect a sound penal policy, the shorter the period of custody the better. 'Short sentences of imprisonment are as good as long sentences', the Advisory Council on the Penal System declared in 1976. The reaction among the criminal court judiciary was positive; for 18 months the prison population palpably lessened. Thereafter the rise has been inexorable, to its unprecedented height of over 80,000 in 2007, with the inevitable resort to police cells. The figures became swollen with the introduction in the Criminal Justice Act 2003 of the indeterminate sentence for public protection, an ill-conceived piece of legislation that is currently unsustainable.

Home Secretaries, up until then, had invariably accepted without demur the sentences of the courts (a tradition broken by Kenneth Clarke in 1989), while privately approving efforts to reduce the nascent prison population. The more recent public spat between New Labour Home Secretaries and the higher judiciary went beyond the natural tension that exists between politicians and judges over penal practice. Its effect on public confidence in criminal justice has been to emphasize a punitiveness perceived to exist in the populace and to stunt the liberal stance towards penal affairs. The advent, on 28 June 2007, of a Secretary of State for Justice and the first Lord Chancellor in the House of Commons was greeted positively by those in the Royal Courts of Justice. It was justified as the new incumbent declared that the Government would not build itself out of the crisis of overcrowding. But it is far from clear how the Secretary of State for Justice is going to end the persistent growth in the prison population. Executive release, discharging a whole raft of prisoners much earlier in their sentences, is the only viable way out of the crisis.

Politicization of crime and punishment had come in the form of both political parties vying with each other for electoral support. The phrase – 'tough on crime, tough on the causes of crime' – attributed to Tony Blair and Jack Straw (in opposition in the mid-1990s), and volubly proclaimed ever since – was pure political rhetoric, designed to curry favour with the electorate, and owed nothing to rational thinking about the place of criminal justice and the penal system in pursuance of governmental obligation to effect crime control. An example of both parties devoting their public policies bending to popular voices was their like attitudes to independent advice on a subject that instinctively calls for rational approach by policy-makers.

The Advisory Council on the Penal System, set up by Roy Jenkins in 1966 (on the unprecedented dissolution of the Royal Commission on the Penal System) was cavalierly abandoned in 1980, along with a string of other advisory bodies. The Council had been a prominent vehicle for penal change, notably as architect of the community service order, the one innovative non-custodial sanction since the creation of probation. Throughout the Thatcher administration, advisers were kept in-house, at that time civil servants in the Home Office who until the 1990s managed to maintain the optimistic approach of earlier administrations. When New Labour came to power in 1997 a brave legislative attempt led by a retired Law Lord and warmly supported by the then Lord Chief Justice (Lord Bingham) to revive the Advisory Council was stubbornly rebuffed by the government. Much of the recent friction generated over criminal justice and penal policy would have been moderated by such a body. Instead, whenever the Blair administration sought independent expert advice it rejected anything that did not accord with the imperious policy of toughness towards criminals, a phrase repeated incidentally in June 1999 by the Prime Minister when Chancellor of the Exchequer. Both political parties see advantage in using criminal justice and penal policy for partisan ends. This is a truly shameful betrayal of the public trust.

The underlying reason for the absence of progress in penal reform has been the politician's unwillingness to formulate, let alone construct any rational philosophy. Inheritors of the Gladstone Committee's twin aims in 1895 of deterrence and rehabilitation, both outmoded shortly after the end of the Second World War, provided no viable replacement. Humane containment or positive custody became the aim of the Prison Service, but no true purpose in the penal disposal of convicted offenders emerged. Response was instinctive at each media outburst. Criminal justice, with its strong adherence to the adversarial system of trial, was only partly amended (if far too frequently visited by Acts of Parliament – 53 in the space of 10 years, compared to the 43 over the period of 100 years, 1895–1995) to cater for demands of civil liberties and an unreformed sentencing framework. Any development of alternative sanctions to immediate imprisonment was always half-hearted and ill-considered. And the lengths of sentences were ratcheted up, despite efforts to curb the discretionary forms of sentences, including a resort to mandatory penalties. Indeed, recent restrictions on the sentencing process of the courts have paradoxically led, even when there was no change in the sentencing maxima, to longer sentences for all crimes. Thus, a life sentence for murder at the time of the abolition of the death penalty in 1965 was, for most convicted murderers, around nine years: today it is likely to be 15. The Criminal Justice Act 2003, in its categories of seriousness, assumes 15 years is the norm. A 'lifer' population in prison – several hundred in 1965 – today runs at about 8,000. It is no exaggeration to say, as the Lord Chief Justice pointedly observed in his Birmingham lecture in March 2007, that the prison system is well on its way to creating a generation of geriatric prisoners – an appalling vista for any prison service.

A new sense of direction in penal treatment was accorded in the 1980s by a brief statement of purpose – namely, helping prisoners to lead law-abiding and useful lives, focusing nowadays on reducing re-offending. A major feature of the Prison Service's contribution to that purpose was the establishment of Fresh Start, a far-reaching programme of ridding the system of prison officer overtime, then running at an average of 15 hours a week. This was replaced by a better basic pay in return for improved efficiency and introduced a responsible management structure in each penal establishment. Taken together with some of the reforms recommended by Lord Woolf in his 1991 report on the Strangeways prison riot, and other prison disturbances, the Prison Service has so far avoided serious prison staff discontent and unrest among prisoners. The current move towards merging prison and probation services in the National Offender Management Service (NOMS) has virtually come to a halt, if not abandonment. Yet overcrowding has so dominated the penal scene that changes for the treatment of life inside have been intensified by the inability to enhance the many facets of imprisonment, not least education and other efforts at providing social skills and industrial training. Too often, the sheer handicap of a prisoner learning to live in a state of captivity, to live peaceably outside in the community, has overborne any positive effects of prison.

How then to re-think a penal philosophy for the twenty-first century? The honest politician needs to be guided to a fundamental re-examination of a civilized society's response to crime. Politicians, no doubt shaping and even inflaming a seemingly popular view, proceed on the assumption that what takes place daily in the Crown Courts of England and Wales is a vital element in the control of crime, and that prison does work to promote that element. It is undeniable that the conviction of a serious offender, resulting in an appropriate penal disposal (in many cases, loss of liberty for terms of imprisonment) is important to the offender's victim(s) – in cases of homicide, secondary victims – the neighbourhood of the criminal event, the local community and the country generally. To the extent that these offenders are put out of circulation, criminal justice is translating the symbolism of the criminal court into practical reality. But the criminal justice system is doing no more than just that. The brutal, perhaps socially unpalatable, truth is that the sentences passed down by our judges have little, if any, impact on the nature and extent of criminal activity in society. Society's need to cut down – or at least contain a low level of – crime will always depend on the political stability of the society, its social system that prevents crime, and the efficiency and effectiveness of the agencies of law enforcement. Since only a fraction of lawbreakers is reported to these agencies, the effects of criminal justice will necessarily be severely restricted. For the few offenders who are detected and prosecuted, the criminal process is defensible in terms of a mode of trial that is fair and even-handed as between the Crown and the accused. The sole aim of the criminal trial is thus to ensure a rightful conviction or acquittal as between prosecution and defence. It is not designed to promote other interests – and it is not capable of delivering anything other than justice to those engaged in criminal proceedings. The public needs to be better informed about the criminal justice system, a task much neglected by Government. Public confidence in the system is vital in achieving the equilibrium that civilized society demands.

Criminal justice is in essence not an instrument of crime control. It has a limited, but important function in proceeding to punish the more serious miscreants in society, and thereby to demonstrate to its citizenry that serious misbehaviour may attract the consequence of punishment – a denunciatory function. To engage in any wider purpose, society will not only punish the wrongdoer but also be punishing itself in going beyond its permissible function and directly injuring itself in managing and operating a prison system that is unsustainable, in principle and in practice. The use of imprisonment is a poor investment as a method of controlling crime, whatever its benefits to the victims and others on whom harm has been inflicted by the individual offender.

What is needed is the production of an adequate historical and political sociology of the ways in which crime – a social construct – is represented culturally and treated responsibly by government in contemporary society. Up until now government's penal policies, if they deserve to be so described, have consistently been a crude exercise in thud and blunder.

An afterthought

The collection of essays was signed off on 27 June 2007, designedly to draw a line under the Blair administration, in the hope that a new era of penal policy might emerge. The hope was altogether too optimistic. On taking up office as Secretary of State for Justice on that very day in June, Jack Straw publicly declared that he could not (and would not try to) buy his way out of the crisis in the prison system; that meant impliedly a halt to the building of new prisons, and expectantly, a move towards dismantling some of the antiquated prison estate. Yet within five months, Mr Straw had accepted the proposal from Lord Carter of Coles that a new 'titan' prison (prospectively no fewer than three titans) would be built, each housing 2,500 prisoners. Overcrowding continues to overwhelm every aspect of the prison system to a point where the managers fear a serious risk to the security and safety of our penal institutions. Until overcrowding is tackled, nothing else can produce the radical change that is dictated. A solution looks to be irremediable, if only because politicians find anathema any drastic reduction in time spent in custody for a whole raft of prisoners inside at present.

References

Advisory Council on the Penal System (ACPS) (1970a) *Detention Centres.* London: HMSO.

—— (1970b) *Non-custodial and Semi-custodial Penalties.* London: HMSO.

—— (1974) *Young Adult Offenders.* London: HMSO.

—— (1978) *Sentences of Imprisonment: A Review of Maximum Penalties.* London: HMSO.

Ashworth, Andrew (1983) *Sentencing and Penal Policy.* London: Weidenfeld.

Committee of Inquiry into the United Kingdom Prison Services (1979) *Report.* (Chairman: Mr Justice May.) Cmnd. 7673. London: HMSO.

Crow, Iain (1979) *The Detention Centre Experiment.* London: NACRO.

Fox, Lionel W. (1934) *The Modern English Prison.* London: Routledge and Kegan Paul.

Fry, Margery (1951) *Arms of the Law.* London: Gollancz, for Howard League.

Galaway, Burt and Joe Hudson, eds (1981) *Perspectives on Crime Victims.* St Louis, Mo.

Hobhouse, Stephen, and A. Fenner Brockway, eds (1922) *English Prisons To-day: Being the Report of the Prison System Enquiry Committee.* Privately printed.

Howard, John (1792) *Prisons and Lazarettos*, Vol. 1: *The State of the Prisons in England and Wales.* 4th edn. Repr. Montclair, NJ: Patterson Smith, 1973.

Howard League for Penal Reform (1970) *Making Amends: Criminals, Victims, and Society.* Chichester: Barry Rose.

References

—— (1976) *No Brief for the Dock: Report of the Howard League Working Party on Custody during Trial.* Chichester: Barry Rose.

Ireland: Committee of Inquiry into the Penal System (1985) *Report.* PL. 3391. Dublin: Stationery Office.

Marshall, Tony, and Martin Walpole (1985) *Bringing People Together: Mediation and Reparation Projects in Great Britain.* Research and Planning Unit Paper 33. London: Home Office.

Martinson, R. (1974) 'What Works: Questions and Answers about Prison Reform'. *Public Interest,* No. 35, Spring.

—— (1979) 'New Findings — New Views'. *Hofstra Law Review,* 7, No. 2, pp. 243ff.

Mayhew, Henry, and John Binney (1862) *The Criminal Prisons of London and Scenes of Prison Life.* New impression, London: Cass, 1968.

Playfair, Giles (1971) *The Punitive Obsession: An Unvarnished History of the English Prison System.* London: Gollancz.

Prisons Committee (1895) *Report.* (Chairman: H. J. Gladstone.) C. 7702. London: HMSO.

Radzinowicz, Sir Leon (1966) *Ideology and Crime.* London: Heinemann.

Radzinowicz, Sir Leon and Roger Hood (1986). *A History of the English Criminal Law and Its Administration from 1750.* Vol. 5: *The Emergence of the Penal Policy.* London: Stevens.

Rose, Gordon (1961) *The Struggle for Penal Reform: The Howard League and Its Predecessors,* London: Stevens.

Ryan, Mick (1983) *The Politics of Penal Reform.* London: Longmans.

Shaw, A. G. L. (1966) *Convicts and the Colonies: A Study of Penal Transportation from Great Britain and Ireland to Australia and Other Parts of the British Empire.* London: Faber and Faber.

Stern, Vivien (1987) *Bricks of Shame: Britain's Prisons.* Harmondsworth: Penguin.

Windlesham, Lord (1981) *Responses to Crime.* Oxford: Clarendon Press, 1987.

Wootton, Barbara (1963) *Crime and the Criminal Law.* Hamlyn Lectures. London: Stevens.

Wright, Martin (1981) 'Crime and Reparation: Breaking the Penal Logjam'. *New Society,* December 10.

—— (1982) *Making Good: Prisons, Punishment, and Beyond.* London: Hutchinsons/Burnett Books.

—— (1987) 'What the Public Wants: Surveys of the General Public, Including Victims'. *Justice of the Peace,* February 14.

112

Index

Index